Titus Maccius Plautus

The Mostellaria of Plautus

Titus Maccius Plautus

The Mostellaria of Plautus

ISBN/EAN: 9783337372026

Printed in Europe, USA, Canada, Australia, Japan

Cover: Foto ©Thomas Meinert / pixelio.de

More available books at **www.hansebooks.com**

THE
MOSTELLARIA OF PLAUTUS,

WITH EXPLANATORY NOTES

BY

E. P. MORRIS,

DRURY COLLEGE, SPRINGFIELD, MO.

𝕭𝖔𝖘𝖙𝖔𝖓:
JOHN ALLYN, PUBLISHER.
1880.

PREFACE.

THE text of this edition follows that given in Ramsay's Mostellaria, which is based upon the Codex Vetus of Camerarius, with corrections from the Codex Decurtatus and the Codex Ursinianus, and from the Milan Palimpsest, wherever that can be read. In a few cases other readings than Ramsay's have been adopted, and in some passages the punctuation has been altered.

The substance of the general Introduction is from Mommsen, and the remarks on the Mostellaria from Lorenz and some other sources. They contain nothing new, but are inserted for the convenience of students.

The notes are mainly from the editions of which a list is given at the end of the book. I have intended to give credit for all notes which are taken without material change from another edition, but some have been so altered that it seemed hardly correct to attribute them to the editor by whom they were suggested. These, with the few which are original, are therefore left unsigned.

No attempt has been made to explain the metres of Plautus, partly because so many points about them are still unsettled, partly because they are too difficult for college students.

I shall be grateful to any one who will notify me of errors which can be corrected.

E. P. MORRIS.

DRURY COLLEGE, SPRINGFIELD, MO.

INTRODUCTION.

THE information which has reached us in regard to the life of Plautus is very scanty. The name by which he is usually known is derived from the Umbrian *plotus,* "splayfoot." His real name was supposed to be Marcus Accius, until Ritschl showed, on the authority of the Milan Palimpsest, that it was Titus Maccius. The MSS. and tradition agree in giving Sarsina or Sassina, in Umbria, as his birthplace. The time of his birth is not absolutely certain, but by a comparison of some scattered allusions in Cicero, Gellius, and a few other writers, Ritschl has fixed the date about 254 B. C. The chief authority for the events of the life of Plautus is a passage in Aulus Gellius, Noct. Att. III. 3, quoted from a lost treatise of Varro. In this passage it is stated that he was employed as a workman in the theatre, that he lost in trade the money thus gained, that he returned to Rome in poverty and earned his living by turning a handmill for a baker, and that, while so employed, he wrote three comedies. Gellius gives the names of two of them, but the plays have not been preserved. The most important points in this statement, the low birth of Plautus and his connection with the stage before he began to write, are abundantly confirmed by internal evidence. The date of his earliest

[margin: Life of Plautus.]

appearance as a translator of comedy is fixed by Ritschl about 224. He died in 184.

The number of plays written by Plautus is not known. About a century after his death as many as one hundred <small>Writings.</small> and thirty passed under his name, though doubts were entertained in regard to the genuineness of many of them, and some critics restricted the number to forty or even to twenty. To remove the uncertainty, a recension of the plays was undertaken by Varro, and the twenty which we now possess, with another, the Vidularia, which has since been lost, were fixed upon by him as undoubtedly authentic; of the rest, a few were accepted on internal evidence, but the greater part were rejected. The authority of Varro in matters relating to early Latin literature gives us sufficient warrant for accepting his conclusion as substantially correct. The uncertainty probably arose from the fact that all comedies, after being presented on the stage, ceased to be the property of the writers and passed into the hands of the managers of the games. It is likely that in this way copies of plays were handed down from one manager to another, and, the names of the authors having been lost, the best of the comedies came to be attributed to the most popular of the early comedians. A somewhat similar relation between the author and the theatre has led, even since the invention of printing, to a like uncertainty in regard to some of the writings of Shakspere.

While the material for the personal life of Plautus is scanty, the more important particulars concerning the state of Roman <small>Spirit of the</small> literature in his time and the manner of putting the <small>comedies.</small> plays upon the stage are within our reach. Such

INTRODUCTION. vii

particulars have an especial value in the study of Plautus; they are, indeed, necessary to a fair appreciation of his comedies or to an understanding of the merits which kept them upon the stage for five centuries. It must be remembered that they were written for the sole purpose of amusing a crowd, which was not critical in literary matters, but which expressed its disapprobation by leaving the actors to go on alone, if the play did not prove entertaining. They were written, too, by a man who knew thoroughly the taste of the audience and the means at his command for satisfying that taste. The plays are for acting, not for reading. It is necessary, therefore, for the reader to assume, as far as possible, the attitude of a listener and spectator, to keep in mind the relative positions of the persons upon the stage, to imagine the tones of voice and the inflections with which the words would be spoken, and the expression and gesture which would accompany them; in short, he must let his fancy supply the "stage business" of the play. Read in this way, the words become thoroughly natural and exhibit great vividness and comic force; without some such attempt to enter into the spirit of the play, the student will entirely miss the real merit of Plautus as a comedian.*

Among the marked characteristics of the Roman people is the absence of original artistic power. This is manifest in sculpture, in architecture, in epic and lyric poetry; but it is nowhere more evident than in the drama. *Greek comedy in Rome.* There were, it is true, the germs of comedy in the rude Fescennine verses, which were chanted alternately by two

---

* The account of the theatre, the audience, and the Greek originals in their relation to Plautus, is taken mainly from Mommsen, Bk. III. Chap. XIV.

singers, and in the Atellana, a flute-song accompanied by gestures, from which, in more favorable circumstances, a national drama might have arisen. But beside the fact that the development of a native school of comedy required a freer enjoyment of life than was natural to the Romans, several causes intervened to check the growth of a Latin drama before it had time to reach maturity. On the one hand, the Romans had, before the time of Plautus, already begun to feel the narrowness of the culture which had sufficed for the early centuries of the Republic, and to desire a broader and better training than their schools afforded. It was to supply this demand that translations of Greek poetry were made for school text-books, and that Greek teachers were employed in the city. On the other hand, the contact with the Greeks of Lower Italy and the influx of foreigners into Rome were having their effect in lowering the seriousness of tone which had formerly prevailed, and in revealing to the people forms of amusement of which they had hitherto been ignorant. Especially among the common people that demoralization of manners and life had begun, which ended in producing the idle rabble of the Empire, fed with the public corn and amused at the public expense. Under the combined influence of such causes, the former acting upon the higher classes, the latter upon the lower orders, the public games underwent a radical change. They had consisted of exhibitions of jugglery and rope-dancing, with the simpler kinds of gymnastics, and of a flute song or pantomime for intellectual diversion, but now gladiators were introduced to take the place of the jugglers, and the flute-song gave way to the regular comedy, imported like the school-books from Greece. The more valuable plays of the age of Pericles depended largely upon personal caricature and political allusion, and would have been unintelligible to a Roman audience, but the New Comedy, which at that time held the stage in Greece, was of a different stamp, and to that the directors of the public games turned to supply their need.

The plays of Menander and Philemon began to appear about the time of the death of Alexander,—a time when political liberty had been lost in Greece, when large motives had ceased to move men, and when society under a surface of great polish and refinement concealed a corrupt and impoverished life. Only a few fragments of the New Comedy have been preserved, and our knowledge of the plots and the delineation of character is obtained largely from the Roman copies, and will be considered later. From the fragments, however, we may form some conception of the tone and spirit of this school. Like Euripides, whom he greatly admired, Menander departed from the older standards and subjects, and based his plays upon common life. He put upon the stage the men and manners of his time, reproducing the witty dialogue which he heard in society, with its nice attention to polished language, its refined courtesy, and its frequent carelessness about the deeper realities. He did not care to go below the surface or to rouse strong feeling. He appealed to an audience of high average cultivation, accustomed to hearing and criticising poetry. Some of the men who listened to his plays had heard Demosthenes and the best of the Attic orators, and had learned to read from Homer. The philosophy of the age, or at least of the poet, was Epicurean, and inculcated an

The New Comedy.

easy acquiescence in the conditions of life, whatever they might be, but it was never degraded by Menander into mere pleasure-seeking. On the contrary, it often rose into an earnest appreciation of the higher truths. At all times it was closely connected with every-day affairs, and as it was expressed in clear and almost epigrammatic form, it has given rise to a number of proverbial sayings, some of them still in current use.

The men who were employed to translate the Greek plays, and prepare them for use on the Roman stage in con-
<small>The translators.</small> nection with the public games, were in nearly every case of low birth and of no social standing. Plautus was the son of a slave or a poor freedman, was accustomed to the life of slaves, and earned his livelihood by hard labor, and neither his natural powers of wit nor his instinctive poetic sense can have quite supplied the place of the cultivated taste, to which the New Comedy was calculated to appeal. Even his knowledge of Greek must have been acquired from conversation rather than from reading, and he shows no acquaintance with Greek writings other than those which he translated. We must expect, therefore, to find that the best elements of the Greek play could not pass through such a medium, and that much of the beauty was lost in the recasting.

But beside his own incapacity to reproduce some of the most valuable characteristics of the Greek, the translator was <small>Restrictions upon translators.</small> further hampered by restrictions arising from the severe police supervision, from the rude construction of the stage and theatre, and from the character of the audience to which the comedies were to be presented.

The change in the public games which led to the introduction of the regular comedy was looked upon with suspicion by the Roman magistrates. They had, perhaps, no definite theory of the duties of a good citizen, but the whole tone of life in the first centuries of the Republic was stern and severe, and the leading men felt an instinctive dislike to the idle amusement of the drama. So while they did not forbid the innovation which naturalized comedy in Rome, they put several embarrassing impediments in its way. For one thing, they refused to allow the erection of a permanent theatre, and though a stone building is supposed to have been erected in 179 B. C., it was taken down when the games were over. The plays themselves, also, were subjected to a rigid censorship, and no allusion of any sort to public men or to government measures was allowed. The poet Naevius suffered imprisonment under the strict libel laws for some stage invectives, and so watchful were the police that in the twenty plays of Plautus, written during the stirring times of the Second Punic War, there is only one distant allusion to the conflict which was then going on within and without the city. It is from this cause that a large number of the comedies contain no reference definite enough to fix the date at which they were produced. Still further, in order to emphasize the fact that comedy was an imported luxury and was only admitted on sufferance, no free Roman appeared as an actor in the time of Plautus, and the poet was forbidden to present his characters as Romans. It was necessary that the play should bear on its face the evidence of its foreign origin. Greek names were therefore retained for the persons, the scene was laid in Greece, the actors wore Greek costumes,

Police supervision.

and several times the poet, with a violent effort to retain the Greek stand-point, speaks of the Romans as *barbari*. Though the immediate effect of such a phrase may have been to raise a laugh, the reason for its use lay in the police censorship.

A second restriction upon the translator arose from the imperfection of the theatre in which the comedies were played. Imperfect stage and scenery. The stage was a large covered building with open front, erected anew for each representation, and destined to be pulled down when the games were over. It presented a street-scene, with the fronts of a few houses projecting from the rear wall, sometimes with gardens or porches before them, and with side-streets leading to the back of the stage. There was no acoustic arrangement to aid the voice of the actor, and no machinery by which the interior of a house could be shown. All the action of the play, therefore, took place in the street. In front of this rough structure, a semicircular space was marked off by a high fence, and was cut into terraces or simply sloped toward the stage. No seats seem to have been provided, but spectators brought stools or benches, and established themselves wherever they could find room. The custom of reserving the best places for senators did not arise until just before the death of Plautus.

The translator was also restricted by the character of the Roman audience. We have seen that the regular comedy The audience. came in as a part of the public games, taking the place of the flute-song and pantomime. It therefore inherited, so to speak, the same audience, made up of the lowest orders of the people. The ruling classes took no interest in it, and the fact, just mentioned, that room was not reserved for senators shows that the senators did not ordinarily attend the performances. Nor were the games, as a whole, at this time, of such a kind as to attract the more sober and intelligent among the middle classes. But the thriftless workmen, the petty tradesmen, and all the swarming idlers and beggars of a great city came to the games and sat as spectators of the comedies. Women and children were admitted, and only slaves seem to have been shut out. Probably the audience was not superior in intelligence to those which attend the more respectable minstrel and variety shows of the present day. There are passages here and there in Plautus, chiefly in the prologues, which show that the spectators conducted themselves in a somewhat disorderly fashion, and that the police had to interfere to allow the play to go on. People came in and went out during the performance, and the crowding for standing-room did not cease when the play began. The fact that an actor sometimes turns in the midst of the dialogue to address an explanation or a joke directly to the spectators, suggests that they may have responded with open criticism of the play or the acting. In such circumstances the poet was compelled to think first of holding his audience, and to put literary excellence in the second place. The epilogue to the Captivi, in which Plautus claims for that comedy the merit of decency and artistic propriety, shows that he felt the restriction, and would have been glad to throw the blame for the low tone of his plays upon the low taste of his hearers.

By such translators, under such police supervision, and for such a public, the plays of the New Comedy were put upon the Roman stage. It is worth while to consider what was lost in the transfer from Greece to Italy, what was retained of the original, and what was added by the Latin poet.

The graceful wit, the polish of manners, the delicate shades of expression which marked the New Comedy, were beauties *Features lost in translation.* of too fragile a sort to bear transportation to the Roman stage. The translators could not feel them, the language could not express them, and the audience could not appreciate them. The Epicurean philosophy, too, which made Menander a favorite with Horace, had, in the time of Plautus, taken no hold in Rome, and if it had been incorporated in the translation, would have been wearisome to the listeners, and would have added to the suspicion with which comedy was regarded by the magistrates. The two leading features of the Greek, then, were lost in translation.

It has been said that the fragments of the Attic comedy of Menander and Philemon are too scanty to give a very distinct *Elements retained. Plots.* idea of the plots or of the delineation of character in the complete plays. But the fact that Plautus and Terence, in other respects so different, agree in these directions, and that Terence acknowledges his obligation to the Greek writers for his plots, makes it quite certain that in these two particulars the Roman comedy followed its original. The plays are very much alike in outline. They usually turn upon the intrigues by which a young man succeeds in outwitting his father, and getting possession of his mistress or avoiding detection in some financial irregularity. The leading character is generally a slave, who acts as confidential adviser to the son, and by his knavery and effrontery brings the difficulties to a happy conclusion. The play is apt to end in a reconciliation between father and son, in the pardon or manumission of the slave, and in a marriage between the young man and his mistress, who proves to be the long-lost daughter of an Athenian citizen. The same scenes recur again and again, and the same machinery of credulous old men, concealed listeners, angry masters, cheating slaves and hungry parasites is used in almost every play. For the characters, too, the Roman play is deeply indebted to the Greek, and these, like the plot, are inclined to be somewhat mechanical. The old men are varieties of two types, — the first, stingy and fretful, suspicious of all about them, and egregiously deceived in spite of their watchfulness; the second, free and easy, full of puns and jokes, sympathizing with the younger men and helping on the roguery of the play. Sometimes the avarice is made most prominent, or the querulous anxiety; occasionally the father is shown in a repentant mood, regretting his previous harshness toward his son; in a few cases the old men have a suggestion of Falstaff. But whatever the variation, it is slight, and the two classes above-mentioned cover nearly all cases. The young men, who play the part of lovers, seem rather pale in comparison with the elaborately drawn heroes of modern fiction. They all devote themselves to their mistresses in a somewhat selfish fashion, exhibit an equal fear of the paternal anger and an equal lack of presence of mind, when troubles rise, and they all, with one consent, put their affairs into the hands of their valets. They might exchange cloaks and names without doing much violence to the unity of the play. The young women are Athenian *hetaerae*, and show no more diversity of disposition than their admirers. It may be noticed, however, that in the Mostellaria there is a very evident distinction,

Characters.

carefully preserved, between Callidamates and Delphium on the one side, and Philolaches and Philematium on the other. But it is when we come to the slave-world that individuality and vividness appear in the delineations. And here it is difficult to determine how much is to be attributed to the original, and how much may be supposed to come from Plautus himself. It is safe to say that the life of the poet had made it easy for him to appreciate and render with great naturalness the infinite variety of character among those who were not compressed into one mold by the force of social standing and public opinion. Whether the suggestions came from Menander or from the experience of Plautus, the spirit is thoroughly natural. Among the slaves the confidential attendant and valet comes first. He shares the pleasures and conducts the plots of his young master, either taking the lead altogether, or prompting to trickery and planning the method of escape, or coming in as the unwilling sharer of the danger, the scape-goat, who bears the anger of the deceived father. In some few places we have the good slave, a model to his fellows, abused by them for his faithfulness, and taking his revenge in sarcastic monologues. In two or three plays a slave from the farm comes upon the stage, dressed in goatskin, the butt of the more fortunate dwellers in the city. In the Aulularia and Rudens the slaves try to pilfer on their own account; in the Menaechmi the slave is his master's guardian and prudent adviser; in the Captivi the devotion of a slave to his master is so real and touching as to be almost tragic; in the Amphitruo is a most vivid picture of a confused and well-meaning coward, and the Stichus concludes with a very pretty and graceful banquet of three slaves. Among the women there is perhaps less variety, but they range between the extremes of a coquettish young house-maid and an old duenna. In several of the plays the parasites occupy a large place, standing just above the slaves in the social scale. They are professional diners-out, who pay for an invitation by puns or by submitting to rough practical jokes. They hang about the market-place in the hope of getting a dinner, and accept the proposal of a patron with the proviso that they are to be excused if any one shall make them a better offer.

There are occasional traces of delicacy and refinement which may be supposed to be due to the influence of the Greek original, or to be the result of the natural good taste of Plautus himself. But beyond this, while the Greek form and dress are retained in obedience to the law against presenting Romans on the stage, the tone of a character or of a whole play is sometimes thoroughly Roman. In total disregard of the fact that the play is supposed to be Greek, names of places in Rome are mentioned and neighboring towns are spoken of, as if the scene were in the city itself. The result is a ludicrous mixture of Greek and Roman names, and of customs from either country. This is doubtless due in part to the carelessness of the translator, but still more to the fact that he did not attempt to retain the Greek spirit of the play, and thought only of evading the police censorship. *Mixture of Greek and Roman elements.*

There remain a few general features of the plays, which are not found in the more exact translations of Terence, and which are certainly to be attributed to Plautus himself. The comic element is largely due to an overflowing current of good-nature, of good-humor, of *fun* *Influence of Plautus in the plays.*

and boisterous frolic. It shows itself frequently in the utter absurdity of the trickery practised by slaves, when plans are made upon the spur of the moment, which afford a temporary relief only to plunge the plotter into a worse predicament at the next turn of affairs; or in the beatings and threats distributed by an angry master; or in the enormous cowardice and perplexity of some braggart slave, who has just been boasting of his exploits in war. The punishments inflicted upon slaves, or more often threatened only, assume in the hands of Plautus a hundred comic shapes. When a slave is loaded with chains, he is an iron-rubber, or an iron-bearing shrub;* if he is tied with ropes, he is a dealer in cords; when he is flogged, he is a bottomless abyss of rods, or an anvil, or a garden well watered with blows, or he is melted by the heat of the scourge. His back is the sheet of paper and the rods are pens, or it is a richly embroidered carpet, or a sieve punctured by the goad. If he steals, and is branded with the word *fur*, he is *literatus*, the man of three letters. A slave who has been flogged and sent in irons to work the grinding-mill, reports that he has been engaged in the iron trade at the mills, as a captain in the hammering department. So also the victim of fraud is treated in a variety of humorous ways. He is shaved, sheared, loaded with lies, disjointed, picked to pieces like old rope, led about by the nose, painted over with tricks, shot at by arrows of deception, molded like a lump of clay, or bitted, bridled and ridden by his deceiver. And often these ideas are compressed into a single graphic word, coined for the occasion, and used as a term of abuse. Equally

* Many of the following examples are from Ramsay, who gives very complete lists in Excurs. XV.–XVII.

rich is the vocabulary of terms of endearment, showered upon the object of affection by some admiring fellow-slave. This form of wit is not keen or brilliant, and the critical judgment may not rate it very high, yet it appeals to a love of fun, which is a part of human nature by no means deserving of condemnation. It is to a very similar overflow of animal spirits that some parts of the Pickwick Papers owe their effect, and a similar spirit of exaggeration on the modern stage has produced the Christmas pantomime and the comic opera.

Apart from the question of literary or artistic merit, the plays of Plautus present a curious and invaluable picture of the meeting of two civilizations, the one in its period *Historical value of the* of decline with all its glory in the past, the other *comedy.* still rising toward its highest point of splendor, but with the possibility of decay already beginning to appear. A large part of the New Comedy must have been quite foreign to Roman manners. In family life, in religious feeling, in philosophy, in the conduct of public affairs, in culture, in all forms of art, and especially in language and literature, the two races stood at very different points of their history. At no other time can they be so well contrasted and compared.

MOSTELLARIA.

The name Mostellaria is derived from *monstrum* through the intermediate form *mostellum*, which, though it does not appear to be found in use, would be a diminutive of *monstrum*. Comp. *liber, libellus, labrum, labellum*. From this comes the adjective *mostellaria* (sc. *fabula*). Such *Name.*

adjective forms stand as titles to the Aulularia, Cistellaria, and Asinaria. Rost suspects that they were given by the grammarians to supply the loss of the real names.

The Greek original of the Mostellaria can be determined only by conjecture, but that points with reasonable certainty The Greek original. to the Phasma of Philemon. Festus, in quoting from this play, twice calls it the Phasma. The plays of Menander and Theognetus bearing that name seem to have had plots different from that of the Mostellaria, while the fact that the Mercator and Trinummus are from Philemon shows that Plautus was accustomed to translating from him.

This play is one of those which cannot be dated with certainty. In I. 1. 41, the phrase *unguenta exotica* is used in Date of the Mostellaria. such a way as to give the impression that foreign perfumes were rare. Pliny the Elder speaks of a decree in the year 189 against the sale of *unguenta exotica*, and it is possible that the words in the play may refer to a fact which would be well known to the audience. Also the reference in II. 1. 79–80 to funeral games, which, in the opinion of Ritschl, had been held in only two instances before the death of Plautus, viz., in 226 and 200, may be an indication that the play was not performed before the earlier date.

There is no prologue to the Mostellaria, as to most of the plays of Plautus. This is the less to be regretted, as Prologue and argument. many of the prologues seem to lessen the interest by revealing too much of the plot. It is, besides, the opinion of most scholars that they are spurious, and belong to the century after the death of Plautus. The arguments in acrostic form, which are prefixed to the plays, were written by some grammarian either in the seventh century of the city, or in the age of the Antonines. They imitate the language of Plautus, but with occasional mistakes.

Several of the names, Phaniscus, Callidamates, Philolaches, and Theuropides, seem to be used only for the sound, to remind the spectators that the play is Greek. Simo is a common name for an old man in comedy. Philematium (from φίλημα) is given for its meaning, "Little Kiss," Küsschen, and the diminutive termination in that and in Delphium is added in accordance with a common Latin custom. Misargurides (from μισέω and ἄργυρος, with patronymic termination), "Money-hater's-son," is an ironical name for the usurer. *Dramatis personae.*

The scene, as in eleven other plays of Plautus, is laid in Athens, and the time of the opening is a little before noon. *Place and time.*

In the Mostellaria, the stage presented two or more houses standing side by side, with small gardens in front of them, and before one, at least, a *vestibulum*. This was a porch, either over the front door between the projecting wings of the house, or in the garden, detached from the rest of the building. Upon the stage stood also an altar, which was originally an evidence of the religious character of the performance, but which in the time of Plautus had become merely one of the stage properties. It is used in several of the plays as a place of refuge. *Stage.*

The costumes were Greek, in accordance with the law which forbade the presentation of a Roman citizen on the stage. The men wore a white sleeveless tunic, over which was thrown the *pallium*, a short robe which was *Dress of actors.*

white in the case of the old men, and of a bright color, purple or red, in the case of the younger men. The slaves, Phaniscus and Tranio, wore over the tunic a short mantle, and probably Grumio had the dress given to rustics, a goat-skin cloak, with a pack and staff. The young women, as *meretrices*, wore a short tunic, covered by a dark or variegated robe.

The division into five acts is retained in this text for convenience, but no such division existed in the time of Plautus. <small>Acts and scenes. Cantica.</small> In this play the stage is vacant only after III. 2, IV. 4, and possibly I. 1. It is not likely, however, that any pause was made at these points. The *tibicen* appears to have played one interlude in each comedy, and this is placed by Lorenz after I. 4, while the feast was continued in pantomime on the stage.

Three *Cantica* or lyrical monologues occur in this play, viz., I. 2, III. 2. 1–21, except lines 11 and 12, and IV. 1. 1–25. These were originally sung by the actor with an accompaniment played by the *tibicen*, but since they required violent exertion of the body and the voice, a singer, *cantor*, was introduced by Livius Andronicus to sing the words, while the actor made the appropriate gesticulation.

T. MACCI PLAVTI MOSTELLARIA.

GRAECA PHASMA.

ARGVMENTVM.

Manumisit emptos suos amores Philolaches,
Omnemque apsente rem suo apsumit patre.
Senem, ut revenit, ludificatur Tranio:
Terrifica monstra dicit fieri in aedibus,
Et inde primum emigratum. Intervenit
Lucripeta faenus faenerator postulans,
Ludusque rursum fit senex: nam mutuom
Acceptum dicit pignus emptis aedibus.
Requirit, quae sint. Ait, vicini proxumi.
Inspectat illas; post se derisum dolet;
Ab sui sodale gnati exoratur tamen.

PERSONAE.

Tranio Servos.
Grvmio Servos.
Philolaches Advlescens.
Philemativm Meretrix.
Scapha Ancilla.
Callidamates Advlescens.
Delphivm Meretrix.
Pver.
Thevropides Senex.
Pediseqvi.
Misargvrides Danista.
Simo Senex.
Phaniscvs Advorsitor.
Advorsitor.
Lorarii.

ACTVS I. SCENA I.

Grvmio. Tranio.

GR. Exi e culina, sis, foras, mastigia,
Qui mi inter patinas exhibes argutias.
Egredere, herilis pernicies, ex aedibus.
Ego pol te ruri, si vivam, ulciscar probe.
Exi, inquam, nidor, e culina.   Quid lates ?   5
TR. Quid tibi, malum, hic ante aedis clamatio est ?
An ruri censes te esse ?   Apscede ab aedibus !
Abi rus ! abi dierecte ! apscede ab ianua !
En, hocine volebas ?   *GR.* Perii, cur me verberas ?
TR. Quia tu vis.   *GR.* Patiar.   Sine modo adveniat
   senex :   10
Sine modo venire salvom, quem apsentem comes.
TR. Nec veri simile loquere nec verum, frutex,
Comesse quemquam ut quisquam apsentem possiet.
GR. Tu, urbanus vero scurra, deliciae popli,
Rus mihi tu obiectas ?   Sane credo, Tranio,   15
Quod te in pistrinum scis actutum tradier.
Cis, hercle, paucas tempestates, Tranio,
Augebis ruri numerum, genus ferratile.
Nunc dum lubet licetque, pota, perde rem,
Corrumpe herilem [filium], adulescentem optumum :   20
Dies noctesque bibite, pergraecamini ;

Amicas emite, liberate: pascite
Parasitos: opsonate pollucibiliter!
Haecine mandavit tibi, quom peregre hinc iit, senex?
Hocine modo hic rem curatam offendet suam?   25
Hocine boni esse officium servi existumas,
Vt heri sui corrumpat et rem et filium?
Nam ego illum corruptum duco, quom his factis studet;
Quo nemo adaeque iuventute ex omni Attica
Antehac est habitus parcus nec magis continens,   30
Is nunc in aliam partem palmam possidet.
Virtute id factum tua et magisterio tuo.
TR. Quid tibi, malum, me, aut quid ego agam, curatio est?
An ruri, quaeso, non sunt, quos cures, bovis?
Lubet potare, amare, scorta ducere: 35
Mei tergi facio haec, non tui, fiducia.
GR. Quam confidenter loquitur! fue!   *TR.* At te Iuppiter
Dique omnes perdant: oboluisti allium,
Germana inluvies, rusticus, hircus, hara suis,
Canes capra commixta!   *GR.* Quid vis fieri?   40
Non omnes possunt olere unguenta exotica,
Si tu oles; neque superior quam herus accumbere,
Neque tam facetis, quam tu vivis, victibus.
Tu tibi istos habeas turtures, piscis, avis;
Sine me alliato fungi fortunas meas.   45
Tu fortunatus; ego miser. Patıunda sunt.
Meum bonum me, te tuum maneat malum.
TR. Quasi invidere mihi hoc videre, Grumio,

ACTVS I. SCENA I. 5

Quia mihi bene est, et tibi male est.   Dignissumum est.
Decet me amare, et te bubulcitarier; 50
Me victitare pulcre, te miseris modis.
GR. O carnuficium cribrum, quod credo fore :
Ita te forabunt patibulatum per vias
Stimulis, si huc reveniat [quam primum] senex.
TR. Qui scis, an tibi istuc eveniat prius quam mihi ? 55
GR. Quia numquam merui : tu meruisti, et nunc meres.
TR. Orationis operam compendi face,
Nisi te mala re magna mactari cupis.
GR. Ervom daturin' estis, bubus quod feram ?
Date aes si non estis.   Agite, porro pergite, 60
Quoniam occepistis ! bibite ! pergraecamini !
Este ! effercite vos ! saginam caedite !
TR. Tace atque abi rus : ego ire in Piraeum volo,
In vesperum parare piscatum mihi.
Ervom tibi aliquis cras faxo ad villam adferat. 65
Quid est ? quid tu me nunc optuere, furcifer ?
GR. Pol tibi istuc credo nomen actutum fore.
TR. Dum interea sic sit, istuc 'actutum' sino.
GR. Ita est ; sed unum hoc scito, nimio celerius
Venire quod molestum est, quam illud quod petas. 70
TR. Molestus ne sis : nunc iam i rus, te amove.
Ne tu erres, hercle, praeterhac mihi non facies moram.
GR. Satin' abiit, neque, quod dixi, flocci existumat ?
Proh di inmortales, opsecro vostram fidem,
Facite, huc ut redeat noster quam primum senex, 75
Triennium qui iam hinc abest, priusquam omnia

Periere, et aedis et ager. Qui nisi huc redit,
Paucorum mensum sunt relictae reliquiae.
Nunc rus abibo : nam eccum herilem filium
Video, corruptum ex adulescente optumo. 80

ACTVS I. SCENA II.

Philolaches.

Recordatus multum et diu cogitavi,
Argumentaque in pectus multa institui
Ego, atque in meo corde, si est quod mihi cor,
Eam rem volutavi et diu disputavi,
Hominem quoius rei, quando natus est, 5
Similem esse arbitrarer simulacrumque habere.
Id repperi iam exemplum.
Novarum aedium esse arbitror similem ego hominem,
Quando hic natus est. Ei rei argumenta dicam.
Atque hoc haud videtur veri simile vobis? 10
At ego id faciam esse ita ut credatis.
Profecto, ita esse ut praedico vera, vincam : atque hoc
    vosmet ipsi,
Scio, proinde uti nunc ego esse autumo,
Quando dicta audietis mea, haud aliter id dicetis.
Auscultate, argumenta dum dico ad hanc rem : 15
Simul gnarures vos volo esse hanc rem mecum.

Aedes quom extemplo sunt paratae, expolitae,
Factae probe, examussim :
Laudant fabrum atque aedes probant ; sibi quisque inde
    exemplum expetunt.
Sibi quisque simile, suo usque sumptu ; operam non par-
    cunt suam.   20
Atque ubi illo inmigrat nequam homo indiligensque
Cum pigra familia, inmundus, instrenuus :
Hic iam aedibus vitium additur, bonae quom curantur
    male.
Atque illud saepe fit : tempestas venit,
Confringit tegulas imbricesque : ibi   25
Dominus indiligens reddere alias nevolt.
Venit imber, lavit parietes : perpluont
Tigna ; putrefacit aer operam fabri :
Nequior factus iam est usus aedium ;
Atque haud est fabri culpa. Sed magna pars   30
Moram hanc induxerunt : si quid numo sarciri potest,
Vsque mantant, neque id faciunt, donicum
Parietes ruont : aedificantur aedes totae denuo.
Haec argumenta ego aedificiis dixi ; nunc etiam volo
Dicere, ut hominis aedium esse similis arbitremini.   35
Primumdum parentes fabri liberum sunt
Et fundamentum supstruont liberorum ;
Extollunt, parant sedulo in firmitatem
Et ut in usum boni et in speciem
Populo sint, sibique aut materiae ne parcunt,   40
Nec sumptus ibi sumptui esse ducunt.

Expoliunt, docent literas, iura, leges, suo sumptu et labore.
Nituntur ut alii sibi esse illorum similis expetant.
Ad legionem quom itum, adminiculum eis danunt
Tum iam aliquem cognatum suum : 45
Eatenus abeunt a fabris. Vbi unum emeritum est sti-
  pendium,
Igitur tum specimen cernitur, quo eveniat aedificatio.
Nam ego ad illud frugi usque et probus fui, in fabrorum
Potestate dum fui.
Posteaquam inmigravi in ingenium meum, 50
Perdidi operam fabrorum ilico oppido.
Venit ignavia, ea mihi tempestas fuit,
Mi adventu suo grandinem, imbremque attulit ;
Haec verecundiam mi et virtutis modum
Deturbavit detexitque a me ilico. 55
Postilla optigere eam negligens fui.
Continuo pro imbre amor advenit in cor meum ;
Is usque in pectus permanavit, permadefecit cor meum.
Nunc simul res, fides, fama, virtus, decusque
Deseruerunt : ego sum in usu factus nimio nequior : 60
Atque edepol (ita haec tigna humide putent) non videor
  mihi
Sarcire posse aedes meas, quin totae perpetuae ruant,
Quin cum fundamento perierint, nec quisquam esse
  auxilio queat.
Cor dolet, quom scio, ut nunc sum, atque ut fui.
Quo neque industrior de iuventute erat, 65
Arte gumnastica, disco, hastis, pila,

Cursu, armis, equo; victitabam volupe;
Parsimonia et duritia discipulinae aliis eram:
Optumi quique expetebant a me doctrinam sibi.
Nunc postquam nihili sum, id vero meopte ingenio repperi. 70

ACTVS I. SCENA III.

PHILEMATIVM. SCAPHA. PHILOLACHES.

PHILEM. Iam pridem ecastor frigida non lavi magis lubenter;
Nec, quom me melius, mea Scapha, rear esse defaecatam.
SC. Eventus rebus omnibus, velut horno messis magna
Fuit. *PHILEM.* Quid ea messis attinet ad meam lavationem?
SC. Nihilo plus, quam lavatio tua ad messim. *PHILOL.* O Venus venusta, 5
Haec illa est tempestas mea, mihi quae modestiam omnem
Detexit, tectus qua fui, quam mihi Amor et Cupido
In pectus perpluit meum; neque iam umquam optigere possum.
Madent iam in corde parietes: periere haec oppido aedes.
PHILEM. Contempla, amabo, mea Scapha, satin' haec me vestis deceat. 10
Volo meo placere Philolachi, meo ocello, meo patrono.

SC. Quid tu te exornas, moribus lepidis quom lepida
   tute es?
Non vestem amatores amant mulieris sed vestis far-
   tum.
PHILOL. Ita me di ament, lepida est Scapha: sapit
   scelesta multum.
Vt lepide res omnes tenet, sententiasque amantum!   15
PHILEM. Quid nunc? *SC.* Quid est? *PHILEM.*
   Quin me aspice et contempla, ut haec me deceat.
SC. Virtute formae id evenit, te ut deceat, quidquid
   habeas.
PHILOL. Ergo hoc ob verbum te, Scapha, donabo ego
   hodie aliqui,
Neque patiar, te istanc gratiis laudasse, quae placet mi.
PHILEM. Nolo ego, te adsentari mihi. *SC.* Nimis tu
   quidem stulta es mulier.   20
Eho mavis vituperarier falso, quam vero extolli?
Equidem pol vel falso tamen laudari multo malo,
Quam vero culpari aut meam speciem alios inridere.
PHILEM. Ego verum amo; verum volo dici mihi, men-
   dacem odi.
SC. Ita tu me ames, ita Philolaches tuus te amet, ut ve-
   nusta es.   25
PHILOL. Quid ais, scelesta? quomodo adiurasti? 'ita
   ego istam amarem'?
Quid? 'istaec me' id cur non additum est? Infecta dona
   facio.
Periisti: quod promiseram tibi dono, perdidisti.

SC. Equidem pol miror, tam catam, tam doctam te et bene eductam,
Non stultam, stulte facere. *PHILEM.* Quin mone, quaeso, si quid erro. 30
SC. Tu ecastor erras, quae quidem illum expectes unum, atque illi
Morem praecipue sic geras, atque alios aspernaris.
Matronae, non meretricium est, unum inservire amantem.
PHILOL. Proh Iuppiter, nam quod malum vorsatur meae domi illud?
Di deaeque omnes me pessumis exemplis interficiant, 35
Nisi ego illam anum interfecero siti, fameque, atque algu.
PHILEM. Nolo ego mihi male te, Scapha, praecipere. *SC.* Stulta es plane,
Quae illum tibi aeternum putes fore amicum et benevolentem.
Moneo ego te: te ille deseret aetate et satietate.
PHILEM. Non spero. *SC.* Insperata accidunt magis saepe, quam quae speres. 40
Postremo, si dictis nequis perduci, ut vera haec credas,
Mea dicta ex factis nosce; rem vides, quae sim et quae fui ante.
Nihilo ego, quam nunc tu, sum amata atque uni modo gessi morem,
Qui pol me, ubi aetate hoc caput colorem commutavit,
Reliquit deseruitque me. Tibi idem futurum credo. 45
PHILOL. Vix comprimor, quin involem illi in oculos stimulatrici.

PHILEM. Solam illi me soli censeo esse oportere opsequentem,
Solam ille me soli sibi suo [argento] liberavit.
PHILOL. Proh di immortales, mulierem lepidam et pudico ingenio !
Bene hercle factum, et gaudeo, mihi nihil esse huius causa. 50
SC. Inscita ecastor tu quidem es. *PHILEM.* Quapropter ? *SC.* Quae istuc cures,
Vt te ille amet. *PHILEM.* Cur, opsecro, non curem ? *SC.* Libera es iam.
Tu iam, quod quaerebas, habes : ille te nisi amabit ultro,
Id, pro capite tuo quod dedit, perdiderit tantum argenti.
PHILOL. Perii hercle, ni ego illam pessumis exemplis enicasso. 55
Illa hanc corrumpit mulierem malesuada vitilena.
PHILEM. Numquam ego illi possum gratiam referre, ut meritus est de me,
Scapha : id tu mihi ne suadeas, ut illum minoris pendam.
SC. At hoc unum facito cogites ; si illum inservibis solum,
Dum tibi nunc haec aetatula est, in senecta male querere. 60
PHILOL. In anginam ego nunc me velim vorti, ut veneficae illi
Fauces prehendam, atque enicem scelestam stimulatricem.
PHILEM. Eundem animum oportet nunc mihi esse, gratum ut impetravi,

Atque olim, priusquam id extudi, quom illi subblandie-
bar.
PHILOL. Divi me faciant, quod volunt, ni ob istam
orationem   65
Te liberasso denuo, et ni Scapham enicasso.
SC. Si tibi sat acceptum est, fore tibi victum sempiter-
num,
Atque illum amatorem tibi proprium futurum in vita:
Soli gerundum censeo morem, et capiundos crines.
PHILEM. Vt fama est homini, exin solet pecuniam in-
venire;   70
Ego si bonam famam mihi servasso, sat ero dives.
PHILOL. Siquidem hercle vendundum est, pater venibit
multo potius,
Quam te, me vivo, umquam sinam egere aut mendicare.
SC. Quid illis futurum est ceteris, qui te amant?
PHILEM. Magis amabunt,
Quom [me] videbunt gratiam referr[e bene mer]enti. 75
PHILOL. Vtinam meus nunc mortuos pater ad me
nuntietur,
Vt ego exheredem meis bonis me faciam, atque haec sit
heres.
SC. Iam ista quidem apsumpta res erit: dies noctesque
estur, bibitur,
Neque quisquam parsimoniam adhibet; sagina plane
est.
PHILOL. In te hercle certum est principium, ut sim
parcus, experiri;   80

Nam neque edes quicquam, neque bibes apud me his
    decem diebus.
PHILEM. Si quid tu in illum bene voles loqui, id loqui
    licebit ;
Nec recte si illi dixeris, iam ecastor vapulabis.
PHILOL. Edepol si summo Iovi vivo argento sacruficas-
    sem,
Pro illius capite quod dedi: numquam aeque id bene
    locassem.   85
Vt videas eam medullitus me amare! Oh, probus homo
    sum :
Quae pro me causam diceret, patronum liberavi.
SC. Video, te nihili pendere prae Philolache omnes
    homines :
Nunc, ne eius causa vapulem, tibi potius adsentabor,
Si acceptum sat habes, tibi fore illum amicum sempi-
    ternum.   90
PHILEM. Cedo mihi speculum et cum ornamentis arcu-
    lam actutum, Scapha,
Ornata ut siem, quom huc veniat Philolaches, voluptas
    mea.
SC. Mulier quae se suamque aetatem spernit, speculo ei
    usus est :
Quid opus est speculo tibi, quae tute speculo speculum
    es maxumum ?
PHILOL. Ob istuc verbum, ne nequiquam, Scapha, tam
    lepide dixeris,   95
Dabo aliquid hodie peculi tibi, Philematium mea.

PHILEM. Suo quique loco viden' capillus satis compositus est commode?

SC. Vbi tu commoda es, capillum commodum esse credito.

PHILOL. Vah, quid illa pote peius quicquam muliere memorarier?

Nunc adsentatrix scelesta est; dudum advorsatrix erat. 100

PHILEM. Cedo cerussam. *SC.* Quid cerussa opus nam? *PHILEM.* Qui malas oblinam.

SC. Vna opera ebur atramento candefacere postules.

PHILOL. Lepide dictum de atramento atque ebore! Euge, plaudo Scaphae.

PHILEM. Tum tu igitur cedo purpurissum. *SC.* Non do: scita es tu quidem;

Nova pictura interpolare vis opus lepidissumum? 105

Non istanc aetatem oportet pigmentum ullum attingere,

Neque cerussam, neque melinum, neque aliam ullam offuciam.

Cape igitur speculum. *PHILOL.* Hei mihi misero: suavium speculo dedit.

Nimis velim lapidem, qui ego illi speculo diminuam caput.

SC. Linteum cape atque exterge tibi manus. *PHILEM.* Quid ita, opsecro? 110

SC. Vt speculum tenuisti, metuo, ne oleant argentum manus:

Ne usquam argentum te accepisse suspicetur Philolaches.

PHILOL. Non videor vidisse lenam callidiorem ullam alteram.
Vt lepide atque astute in mentem venit de speculo malae!
PHILEM. Etiamne unguentis unguendam censes? *SC.* Minume feceris. 115
PHILEM. Quapropter? *SC.* Quia ecastor mulier recte olet, ubi nihil olet.
Nam istaec veteres, quae se unguentis unctitant, interpoles,
Vetulae, edentulae, quae vitia corporis fuco occulunt,
Vbi sese sudor cum unguentis consociavit, ilico
Itidem olent, quasi quom una multa iura confudit cocus: 120
Quid oleant, nescias, nisi id unum, ut male olere intellegas.
PHILOL. Vt perdocte cuncta callet! nihil hac docta doctius!
Verum illud esse maxuma adeo pars vostrorum intellegit,
Quibus anus domi sunt uxores, quae vos dote meruerunt.
PHILEM. Agedum, contempla aurum et pallam, satin' haec me deceat, Scapha. 125
SC. Non me curare istuc oportet. *PHILEM.* Quem, opsecro, igitur? *SC.* Eloquar.
Philolachem: is ne quid emat nisi quod tibi placere censeat.
Nam amator meretricis mores sibi emit auro et purpura:
Quid opus est, quod suum esse nolit, ei ultro ostentarier?

Purpura aetas occultanda est; aurum turpe mulieri.   130
Pulcra mulier nuda erit, quam purpurata, pulcrior:
Postea nequiquam exornata est bene, si morata est male:
Pulcrum ornatum turpes mores peius caeno conlinunt.
Nam si pulcra est, nimis ornata est. *PHILOL.* Nimis diu apstineo manum.
Quid hic vos duae agitis? *PHILEM.* Tibi me exorno ut placeam. *PHILOL.* Ornata es satis.   135
Abi tu hinc intro, atque ornamenta haec aufer. — Sed, voluptas mea,
Mea Philematium, potare tecum conlubitum est mihi.
PHILEM. Lubet et edepol mihi tecum: nam quod tibi lubet, idem mihi lubet,
Mea voluptas. *PHILOL.* Hem, istuc verbum vile est viginti minis.
PHILEM. Cedo, amabo, decem: bene emptum tibi dare hoc verbum volo.   140
PHILOL. Etiam nunc decem minae apud te sunt: vel rationem puta:
Triginta minas pro capite tuo dedi — *PHILEM.* Cur exprobras?
PHILOL. Egone id exprobrem? Quin mihimet cupio id opprobrarier;
Nec quicquam argenti locavi iam diu usquam aeque bene.
PHILEM. Certe ego, quod te amo, operam nusquam melius potui ponere.   145*

PHILOL. Bene igitur ratio accepti atque expensi inter
    nos convenit :
Tu me amas, ego te amo ; merito id fieri uterque existu-
    mat.
Haec qui gaudent, gaudeant perpetuo suo semper bono ;
Qui invident, ne umquam eorum quisquam invideat pro-
    sus commodis.
PHILEM. Age, accumbe igitur.— Cedo aquam manibus,
    puer. Appone hic mensulam.   150
Vide, tali ubi sint. — Vin' unguenta ? *PHILOL.* Quid
    opus est ? Cum stacta accubo.
Sed estne hic meus sodalis, qui huc incedit cum amica
    sua ?
Is est Callidamates ; cum amica, eccum, incedit. Euge,
    oculus meus,
Conveniunt manuplares, eccos ; praedam participes pe-
    tunt.

ACTVS I. SCENA IV.

CALLIDAMATES. DELPHIVM. PHILOLACHES. PHILE-
MATIVM.

CA. Advorsum venire mihi ad Philolachem
Volo temperi ; audi : hem, tibi imperatum est.
Nam illi, ubi fui, inde effugi foras :
Ita me ibi male convivi sermonisque taesum est.

Nunc commissatum ibo ad Philolachetem, 5
Vbi nos hilari ingenio et lepide accipiet.
Ecquid tibi videor ma-ma-madere?
DE. Semper istoc modo moratus, vita, debebas —
CA. Visne ego te ac tu me amplectare?
DE. Si tibi cordi est·facere, licet. *CA.* Lepida es. 10
Duce me, amabo. *DE.* Cave ne cadas. Asta.
CA. Oh! oh! ocellus es meus; tuus sum alumnus, mel
  meum.
DE. Cave modo, ne prius in via accumbas,
Quam illi, ubi lectus est stratus, coimus.
CA. Sine sine cadere me. *DE.* Sino. *CA.* Sed et hoc,
  quod mihi in manu est. 15
DE. Si cades, non cades, quin cadam tecum.
Iacentis tollet postea nos ambos aliquis.
Madet homo. *CA.* Tun' me ais ma-ma-madere?
DE. Cedo manum: nolo equidem te adfligi.
CA. Hem, tene. *DE.* Age, i i simul. *CA.* Quo ego
  eam, an scis? 20
DE. Scio. *CA.* In mentem venit modo: nempe domum
  eo
Commissatum. *DE.* Imo— *CA.* Istuc quidem iam
  memini.
PHILOL. Num non vis me obviam his ire, anime mi?
Illi ego ex omnibus optume volo.
Iam revortar. *PHILEM.* Diu 'iam' id mihi. 25
CA. Ecquis hic est? *PHILOL.* Adest. *CA.* Eu,
  Philolaches,

Salve, amicissume mihi omnium hominum.
PHILOL. Di te ament.   Accuba, Callidamates.
Vnde agis te?   *CA.* Vnde homo ebrius.
PHILOL. Probe.   Quin amabo accubas, Delphium
    mea? 30
CA. Da illi, quod bibat; dormiam ego iam.
PHILOL. Num mirum aut novom quippiam facit?
Quid ego hoc faciam postea, mea? *DE.* Sic sine eumpse.
PHILOL. Age tu, interim da ab Delphio cito cantherum
    circum.

ACTVS II. SCENA I.

TRANIO. PHILOLACHES. CALLIDAMATES. DELPHIVM.
PHILEMATIVM. PVER.

TR. Iuppiter supremus summis opibus atque industriis,
Me perisse et Philolachetem cupit, herilem filium.
Occidit spes nostra : nusquam stabulum est confidentiae,
Nec Salus nobis saluti iam esse, si cupiat, potest :
Ita mali maeroris montem maxumum ad portum modo 5
Conspicatus sum : herus advenit peregre : periit Tranio.
Ecquis homo est, qui facere argenti cupiat aliquantum
    lucri,
Qui hodie sese excruciari meam vicem possit pati?
Vbi sunt isti plagipatidae, ferritribaces viri,
Vel isti, qui trium numorum causa subeunt sub falas, 10

Vbi aliqui quindenis hastis corpus transfigi solent?
Ego dabo ei talentum, primus qui in crucem excucurrerit;
Sĕd ea lege, ut offigantur bis pedes, bis braohia.
Vbi id erit factum, a me argentum petito praesentarium.
Sed ego sumne ille infelix, qui non curro curriculo do-
    mum?   15
PHILOL. Adest opsonium: eccum, Tranio a portu
    redit.
TR. Philolaches! *PHILOL.* Quid est? *TR.* [Et]
    ego et tu— *PHILOL.* Quid 'et ego et tu'?
TR. Perimus!
PHILOL. Quid ita? *TR.* Pater adest. *PHILOL.*
    Quid ego ex ted audio? *TR.* Apsumpti sumus.
Pater, inquam, tuus venit. *PHILOL.* Vbi is est, opsecro
    te? *TR.* Adest. *PHILOL.* [Adest?]
Quis id ait? quis vidit? *TR.* Egomet, inquam, vidi.
    PHILOL. Vae mihi!   20
Quid ego ago? *TR.* Nam quid tu, malum, me rogitas,
    quid agas? Accubas.
PHILOL. Tun' vidisti? *TR.* Egomet, inquam.
    PHILOL. Certe? *TR.* [Certe,] inquam. *PHI-
    LOL.* Occidi,
Si tu vera memoras. *TR.* Quid mihi sit boni, si men-
    tiar?
PHILOL. Quid ego nunc faciam? *TR.* Iube haec hinc
    omnia amolirier.
Quis istic dormit? *PHILOL.* Callidamates. *TR.* Sus-
    cita istum, Delphium.   25

DE. Callidamates, Callidamates, vigila! *CA.* Vigilo:
　　cedo ut bibam.
DE. Vigila: pater advenit peregre Philolachae. *CA.* Va-
　　leat pater.
PHILOL. Valet ille quidem; atque [ego] disperi. *CA.*
　　Bis peristi? Qui potest?
PHILOL. Quaeso edepol, exsurge: pater advenit. *CA.*
　　Tuus venit pater?
Iube abire rursum. Quid illi reditio huc etiam fuit? 30
PHILOL. Quid ego agam? Pater iam hic me offendet
　　miserum adveniens ebrium,
Aedis plenas convivarum et mulierum. Miserum est
　　opus,
Igitur demum fodere puteum, ubi sitis fauces tenet;
Sicut ego adventu patris nunc quaero, quid faciam miser.
TR. Ecce autem, hic deposivit caput, et dormit. Sus-
　　cita.　　　　　　　　　　　　　　　　　　　　　35
PHILOL. Etiam vigilas? Pater, inquam, aderit iam
　　hic meus. *CA.* Ain' tu, pater?
Cedo soleas mihi, ut arma capiam! iam pol ego occidam
　　patrem.
PHILOL. Perdis rem: tace. Amabo, abripite hunc
　　intro actutum inter manus.
CA.　　*　*　*　*　*　*　*　*　*
PHILOL. Perii! *TR.* Habe bonum animum: ego is-
　　tum lepide medicabo metum.　　　　　　　　40
PHILOL. Nullus sum! *TR.* Taceas: ego, qui istaec
　　sedem, meditabor, tibi.

ACTVS II. SCENA I.   23

Satin' habes, si ego advenientem ita patrem faciam tuum,
Non modo ne intro eat, verum etiam ut fugiat longe ab
    aedibus?
Vos modo hinc abite intro atque haec hinc propere
    amolimini.
PHILOL. Vbi ego ero? *TR.* Vbi maxume esse vis:
    cum hac, cum istac eris.   45
DE. Quid est igitur? abeamus hinc nos? *TR.* Non
    hoc longe, Delphium.
Nam intus potate haud tantillo hac quidem causa minus.
PHILOL. Ei mihi, quam, istaec blanda dicta quo eveni-
    ant, madeo metu!
TR. Potin', animo ut sies quieto et facias, quod iubeo?
    PHILOL. Potest.
TR. Omnium primum Philematium, intro abi, et tu, Del-
    phium.   50
DE. Morigerae tibi erimus ambae. *TR.* Ita ille faxit
    Iuppiter!
Animum advorte nunc tu iam, quae volo accurarier.
Omnium primumdum aedes iam face occlusae sient.
Intus cave muttire quemquam siveris. *PHILOL.* Cu-
    rabitur.
TR. Tamquam si intus natus nemo in aedibus habitet.
    PHILOL. Licet.   55
TR. Neu quisquam responset, quando hasce aedis pulta-
    bit senex.
PHILOL. Numquid aliud? *TR.* Clavem mi harunce
    aedium Laconicam

Iam iube efferri intus : hasce ego aedis occludam hinc
 foris.
PHILOL. In tuam custodiam meque et spes meas trado,
 Tranio.
TR. Pluma haud interest, patronus an cluens proprior
 siet   60
Homini, quoi nulla in pectore est audacia.
Nam quoivis homini, vel optumo vel pessumo,
Quamvis desubito facile est facere nequiter;
Verum id videndum est, id viri docti est opus,
Quae designata sint et facta nequitia,   65
Tranquille cuncta et ut proveniant sine malo :
Ni quid patiatur, quamobrem pigeat vivere :
Sicut ego efficiam, quae facta hic turbavimus,
Profecto ut liqueant omnia et tranquilla sint,
Nec quicquam nobis pariant ex se incommodi.   70
Sed quid tu egrederis ? Perii ! — o, iamiam optume
Praeceptis paruisti ! *PVER.* [Herus] iussit maxumo
Opere orare, ut patrem aliquo apsterreres modo,
Ne introiret aedis. *TR.* Quin etiam illi hoc dicito,
Facturum, ut ne etiam aspicere aedis audeat,   75
Capite obvoluto ut fugiat, cum summo metu.
Clavim cedo atque abi hinc intro, atque occlude ostium,
Et ego hinc occludam. — Iube venire nunc iam !
Ludos ego hodie vivo praesenti hic seni
Faciam, quod credo mortuo numquam fore.   80
Concedam a foribus huc ; hinc speculabor procul,
Vnde advenienti sarcinam inponam seni.

ACTVS II. SCENA II.

THEVROPIDES. PEDISEQVI. TRANIO.

TH. Habeo, Neptune, gratiam magnam tibi,
Quom me amisisti a te vix vivom modo!
Verum si posthac me pedem latum modo
Scies inposisse in undam : haud causa ilico est,
Quod nunc voluisti facere, quin facias mihi. 5
Apage, apage te a me nunc iam post hunc diem ;
Quod crediturus tibi fui, omne credidi.
TR. Edepol, Neptune, peccavisti largiter,
Qui occasionem hanc amisisti tam bonam.
TH. Triennio post Aegupto advenio domum. 10
Credo, expectatus veniam familiaribus.
TR. Nimio edepol ille potuit expectatior
Venire, qui te nuntiaret mortuom.
TH. Sed quid hoc ?   Occlusa ianua est interdius ?
Pultabo.   Heus, ecquis istas aperit mihi fores ? 15
TR. Quis homo est, qui nostras aedes accessit prope ?
TH. Meus servos hic quidem est Tranio.   *TR.* O Theu-
    ropides,
Here, salve : salvom te advenisse gaudeo.
Vsque invaluisti ?   *TH.* Vsque, ut vides.   *TR.* Factum
    optume.
TH. Quid vos ? insanin' estis ?   *TR.* Quidum ?   *TH.*
    Sic : quia 20

Foris ambulatis ; natus nemo in aedibus
Servat, neque qui recludat, neque qui respondeat.
Pultando pene confregi hasce ambas foris.
TR. Eho an tu tetigisti has aedis ?   *TH.* Cur non tan-
   gerem ?
Quin pultando, inquam, pene confregi foris.   25
TR. Tetigistin' ?   *TH.* Tetigi, inquam, et pultavi.   *TR.*
   Vah!   *TH.* Quid est ?
TR. Male hercle factum !   *TH.* Quid est negoti?   *TR.*
   Non potest
Dici, quam indignum facinus fecisti et malum.
TH. Quid iam ?   *TR.* Fuge, opsecro, atque apscede ab
   aedibus.
Fuge huc, fuge ad me proprius !   Tetigistin' fores ?   30
TH. Quomodo pultare potui, si non tangerem ?
TR. Occidisti hercle —   *TH.* Quem mortalem ?   *TR.*
   Omnis tuos.
TH. Di te deaeque omnis faxint cum isto omine —
TR. Metuo, te atque istos expiare ut possies.
TH. Quamobrem, aut quam subito rem mihi adportas
   novam ?   35
TR. Et, heus, iube illos illinc, amabo, apscedere.
TH. Apscedite.   *TR.* Aedes ne attigatis !   Tangite
Vos quoque terram !   *TH.* Opsecro hercle, quin eloquere
   [iam].
TR. Quia septem menses sunt, quom in hasce aedis
   pedem
Nemo intro tetulit, semel ut emigravimus.   40

TH. Eloquere, quid ita? *TR.* Circumspicedum, num quis est,
Sermonem nostrum qui aucupet. *TH.* Tutum probe est.
TR. Circumspice etiam. *TH.* Nemo est: loquere nunc iam.
TR. Capitalis caedis facta est. *TH.* Non intellego.
TR. Scelus, inquam, factum est iamdiu, antiquom et vetus. 45
Antiquom; id adeo nos nunc factum invenimus.
TH. Quid istuc est scelus, aut quis id fecit, cedo.
TR. Hospes necavit hospitem captum manu;
Iste, ut ego opinor, qui has tibi aedis vendidit.
TH. •Necavit? *TR.* Aurumque ei ademit hospiti, 50
Eumque hic defodit hospitem ibidem in aedibus.
TH. Quapropter id vos factum suspicamini?
TR. Ego dicam: ausculta. Vt foris cenaverat
Tuus gnatus, postquam redit a cena domum:
Abimus omnes cubitum, condormivimus. 55
Lucernam forte oblitus fueram extinguere:
Atque ille exclamat derepente maxumum.
TH. Quis homo? an gnatus meus? *TR.* St! tace; ausculta modo.
Ait, venisse illum in somnis ad se mortuom.
TH. Nempe ergo in somnis? *TR.* Ita. Sed ausculta modo. 60
Ait illum hoc pacto sibi dixisse mortuom —
TH. In somnis? *TR.* Mirum, quin vigilanti diceret,
Qui abhinc sexaginta annis occisus foret.

Interdum inepte stultus es. *TH.* Taceo. *TR.* Sed ecce,
    quae ille inquit:
" Ego transmarinus hospes sum Diapontius ;   65
Hic habito; haec mihi dedita est habitatio:
Nam me Acheruntem recipere Orcus noluit,
Quia praemature vita careo. Per fidem
Deceptus sum : hospes me hic necavit, isque me
Defodit insepultum clam in hisce aedibus,   70
Scelestus, auri causa. Nunc tu hinc emigra:
Scelestae hae sunt aedes, impia est habitatio."
Quae hic monstra fiunt, anno vix possum eloqui.
St, st! *TH.* Quid, opsecro, hercle, factum est? *TR.*
    Concrepuit foris.
Hicine percussit? *TH.* Guttam haud habeo sangui-
    nis.   75
Vivom me accersunt ad Acheruntem mortui.
TR. Perii! illisce hodie hanc conturbabunt fabulam.
Nimis quam formido, ne manufesto hic me opprimat.
TH. Quid tute tecum loquere? *TR.* Apscede ab ianua.
Fuge, opsecro hercle! *TH.* Quo fugiam? Etiam tu
    fuge.   80
TR. Nil ego formido: pax mihi est cum mortuis.
TH. Heus, Tranio! *TR.* Non me appellabis, si sapis:
Nihil ego commerui, neque istas percussi fores.
TH. Quaeso, quid aegre est? quae res te agitat, Tranio?
Quicum istaec loquere? *TR.* An, quaeso, tu appella-
    veras?   85
Ita me di amabunt, mortuom illum credidi

Expostulare, quia percussisses fores.
Sed tu etiamne astas, nec, quae dico, optemperas?
TH. Quid faciam? *TR.* Cave respexis, fuge, operi
    caput!
TH. Cur non fugis tu? *TR.* Pax mihi est cum mor-
    tuis.   90
TH. Scio. Quid modo igitur? cur tanto opere extimu-
    eras?
TR. Nil me curassis, inquam: ego mihi providero;
Tu, ut occepisti, tantum quantum quis, fuge;
Atque Herculem invocabis. *TH.* Hercules, te invoco!
TR. Et ego, tibi hodie ut det, senex, magnum malum. 95
Proh di immortales, opsecro vostram fidem,
Quid ego hodie negoti confeci malum!

ACTVS III. SCENA I.

DANISTA. THEVROPIDES. TRANIO.

DA. Scelestiorem ego annum argento faenori
Numquam ullum vidi, quam hic mihi annus optigit.
·A mani ad noctem usque in foro dego diem;
Locare argenti nemini numum queo.
TR. Nunc pol ego perii plane in perpetuom modum: 5
Danista adest qui dedit [argentum faenori]
Qui amica est empta, quoque [opus in sumptus fuit].

Manufesta res est, nisi quod occurro prius,
Ne hoc [nunc] senex resciscat. Ibo huic obviam.
Sed quidnam hic sese tam cito recipit domum ?   10
Metuo, ne de hac re quidpiam indaudiverit.
Accedam atque adpellabo. Hei, quam timeo miser !
Nihil est miserius, quam animus hominis conscius,
Sicut me habet. Verum utut res sese habet,
Pergam turbare porro : ita haec res postulat.   15
Vnde is ? *TH.* Conveni illum, unde hasce aedis emeram.
TR. Numquid dixisti de illo, quod dixi tibi ?
TH. Dixi hercle vero [illi] omnia. *TR.* Vae misero
    mihi !
Metuo, ne techinae meae perpetuo perierint !
TH. Quid tute tecum ? *TR.* Nihil enim. Sed dic
    mihi :   20
Dixtine, quaeso ? *TH.* Dixi, inquam, ordine omnia.
TR. Etiam fatetur de hospite ? *TH.* Imo pernegat.
TR. Negat ? [*TH.* Negat, inquam. *TR.* Perii oppido,]
    quom cogito.
[Non confitetur ?] *TH.* Dicam si confessus sit.
Quid nunc faciundum censes ? *TR.* Egon' quid cen-
    seam ?   25
Cape, opsecro hercle [te], cum eo una iudicem ;
Sed eum videto ut capias, qui credat mihi :
Tam facile vinces, quam pirum volpes comest.
DA. Sed Philolachetis servom eccum Tranium ;
Qui mihi neque faenus neque sortem argenti danunt. 30
TH. Quo te agis ? *TR.* Nec quoquam abeo. — Nam
    ego sum miser,

Scelestus, natus dis inimicis omnibus.
Iam illo praesente adibit.   Ne ego homo sum miser :
Ita et hinc et illinc mi exhibent negotium.
Sed occupabo adire. *DA.* Hic ad me it : salvos sum : 35
Spes est de argento.   *TR.* Hilarus est.   Frustra est
    homo.
Salvere iubeo te, Misargurides, bene.
DA. Salve et tu.   Quid de argento est ?   *TR.* Abi, sis,
    belua !
Continuo adveniens pilum iniecisti mihi.
DA. Hic homo est inanis.   *TR.* Hic homo certe est
    hariolus.   .   40
DA. Quin tu istas mittis tricas ?   *TR.* Quin, quid vis,
    cedo.
DA. Vbi Philolaches est ?   *TR.* Numquam potuisti mihi
Magis opportunus adven[ire, quam] advenis.
DA. Quid est ?   *TR.* Concede huc.   [*DA.* Quin mihi
    argentum red]ditur ?
TR. Scio te bona esse voce : [ne clama nimis.]   45
DA. Ego hercle vero clamo.   *TR.* Ah, gere morem
    mihi.
DA. Quid tibi ego morem vis geram ?   *TR.* Abi, quaeso,
    hinc domum.
DA. Abeam ?   *TR.* Redito huc circiter meridiem.
DA. Reddeturne igitur faenus ?   *TR.* Reddetur.   Abi.
DA. Quid ego huc recursem, aut operam sumam aut
    conteram ?   50
Quid si hic manebo potius ad meridiem ?

TR. Imo abi domum.   Verum hercle dico.   Abi modo.
DA. Quin vos mihi faenus date.   Quid hic nugamini?
TR. Eu hercle! — Ne tu abi modo; ausculta mihi.
DA. Iam hercle ego illunc nominabo.   *TR.* Euge strenue!   55
Beatus vero es nunc, quom clamas.   *DA.* Meum peto.
Multos me hoc pacto iam dies frustramini.
Molestus si sum, reddite argentum: abiero.
Responsiones omnes hoc verbo eripis.
TR. Sortem accipe.   *DA.* Imo faenus: id primum volo.   60
TR. Quid ais tu? omnium hominum teterrume,
Venisti huc te extentatum?   Agas, quod in manu est.
Non dat: non debet.   *DA.* Non debet?   *TR.* Ne γρῦ quidem
Ferre hinc potes; an [mavis ut ali]quo abeat foras,
Vrbem exul [linquat factus] hic causa tui?   65
Quoi sortem [vix dare] licebit?   *DA.* Quin non peto.
Mihi faenus reddat, faenus actutum mihi.
TR. Molestus ne sis; nemo dat; age, quod lubet.
Tu solus, credo, faenore argentum datas.
DA. Cedo faenus! redde faenus! faenus reddite!   70
Daturin' estis faenus actutum mihi?
Date mihi faenus!   *TR.* Faenus illic, faenus hic!
Nescit quidem nisi faenus fabularier
[Veterator; neque] ego tetriorem beluam
Vidisse me umquam quemquam, quam te, censeo.   75
DA. Non edepol nunc me tu istis verbis territas.
TH. Quod illuc est faenus, opsecro, quod illic petit?

ACTVS III. SCENA I.

TR. Pater eccum advenit peregre non multo prius
Illius; is tibi et faenus et sortem dabit:
Ne inconciliare quid nos porro postules. 80
Vide, num moratur. *DA.* Quin feram, si quid datur.
TH. Quid ais tu? *TR.* Quid vis? *TH.* Quis illic
 est? quid illic petit?
Quid Philolachetem gnatum compellat [meum]
Sic, et praesenti tibi facit convicium?
Quid illi debetur? *TR.* Opsecro hercle iube 85
Obici argentum ob os impurae beluae.
TH. Iubeam? *TR.* Iube homini argento os ver-
 berarier.
DA. Perfacile ego ictus perpetior argenteos.
TR. Audin? videtur, opsecro hercle, idoneus,
Danista qui sit, genus quod improbissumum est? 90
TH. Non ego [nunc] istuc curo, qui sit, unde sit:
Id volo mihi dici, id me scire expeto,
Quod illud argentum est. *TR.* Est — huic debet Philo-
 laches
Paulum. *TH.* Quantillum? *TR.* Quasi quadraginta
 minas.
DA. Ne sane id multum censeas; paulum id quidem
 est. 95
TH. Adeo etiam argenti faenus creditum audio.
TR. Quatuor quadraginta illi debentur minae,
Et sors et faenus. *DA.* Tantum est; nihilo plus peto.
TR. Velim quidem hercle, ut uno numo plus petas.
Dic te daturum, ut abeat. *TH.* Ego dicam dare? 100

TR. Dic. *TH.* Egone? *TR.* Tu ipsus. Dic modo!
 ausculta mihi!
Promitte! age, inquam: ego iubeo. *TH.* Responde mihi:
Quid eo est argento factum? *TR.* Salvom est. *TH.*
 Solvite
Vosmet igitur, si salvom est. *TR.* Aedes filius
Tuus emit. *TH.* Aedis? *TR.* Aedis. *TH.* Euge,
 Philolaches 105
Patrissat! iam homo in mercatura vortitur.
Ain' tu, aedis? *TR.* Aedis, inquam. Sed scin', quoius-
 modi?
TH. Qui scire possim? *TR.* Vah! *TH.* Quid est?
 TR. Ne me roga.
TH. Nam quid ita? *TR.* Speculo claras, clarorem me-
 rum.
TH. Bene hercle factum! Quid? eas quanti desti-
 nat? 110
TR. Talentis magnis totidem, quot ego et tu sumus.
Sed arraboni has dedit quadraginta minas.
Hinc sumpsit, quas ei dedimus. Satin' intellegis?
Nam postquam haece aedis ita erant, ut dixi tibi,
Continuo est alias aedis mercatus sibi. 115
TH. Bene hercle factum! *DA.* Heus, iam adpetit me-
 ridies.
TR. Apsolve hunc, quaeso, vomitum; ne hic nos
 enecet.
TH. Adulescens, mecum rem habe. *DA.* Nempe aps
 te petam?

TH. Petito cras. *DA.* Abeo: sat habeo, si cras fero.
TR. Malum — quod isti di deaeque omnes duint: 120
Ita mea consilia perturbat penissume.
Nullum edepol hodie genus est hominum tetrius
Nec minus bono cum iure, quam danisticum.
TH. Qua in regione istas aedis emit filius?
TR. Ecce autem perii! *TH.* Dicisne hoc, quod te
    rogo? 125
TR. Dicam; sed nomen domini quaero quid siet.
TH. Age, comminiscere ergo. *TR.* Quid ego nunc agam,
Nisi ut in vicinum hunc proxumum mendacium?
Eas emisse aedis huius dicam filium.
Calidum hercle audivi esse optumum mendacium; 130
Calidum hoc est: etsi procul abest, urit male.
Quidquid dei dicunt, id rectum est dicere.
TH. Quid igitur? iam commentus? *TR.* Di istum
    perduint!
— Imo istunc potius! — De vicino hoc proxumo
Tuus emit aedis filius. *TH.* Bonan' fide? 135
TR. Si quidem es argentum redditurus, tum bona;
Si redditurus non es, non emit bona.
TH. Non in loco emit perbono. *TR.* Imo in optumo.
TH. Cupio hercle inspicere hasce aedis: pultadum fores,
Atque evoca aliquem intus ad te, Tranio. 140
TR. Ecce autem iterum nunc, quid dicam, nescio.
Iterum iam ad unum saxum me fluctus ferunt.
Quid nunc? Non hercle, quid nunc faciam, reperio;
Manufesto teneor. *TH.* Evocadum aliquem ocius:

Roga circumducat. *TR.* Heus tu!— At hic sunt mu-
    lieres: 145
Videndum est primum, utrum eae velintne, an non velint.
TH. Bonum aequomque oras : percontare et roga.
Ego hic tantisper, dum exis, te opperiar foris.
TR. Di te deaeque omnis funditus perdant, senex :
Ita mea consilia undique oppugnas male. 150
Euge, optume, eccum, aedium dominus foras
Simo progreditur ipsus. Huc concessero,
Dum mihi senatum consili in cor convoco :
Igitur tum accedam hunc, quando quid agam invenero.

ACTVS III. SCENA II.

Simo. Thevropides. Tranio.

SI. Melius anno hoc mihi non fuit domi,
Nec quod una esca me iuverit magis.
Prandium uxor mihi perbonum dedit ;
Nunc dormitum iubet me ire. Minume!
Non mihi forte visum ilico fuit, 5
Melius quom prandium, quam solet, dedit:
Voluit in cubiculum abducere me anus.
Non bonum est somnium de prandio ; apage!
Clanculum ex aedibus me edidi foras.
Tota turget mihi uxor scio [nunc] domi. 10

ACTVS III. SCENA II.

TR. Res parata est mala in vesperum huic seni:
Nam et cenandum ei et cubandum est male.
SI. Quom magis cogito cum meo animo:
Si quis dotatam uxorem atque anum habet,
Neminem sollicitat sopor: ibi omnibus 15
Ire dormitum odio est, velut nunc mihi.
Exsequi certa res est, ut abeam
Potius hinc ad forum, quam domi cubem.
Atque pol nescio ut moribus sient
Vostrae: haec, sat scio, quam me habeat male; 20
Peius posthac fore, quam fuit, mihi.
TR. [Si] abitus tuus tibi, senex, fecerit male,
Nihil erit, quod deorum ullum accusites;
Te ipse iure optumo merito incuses licet.
Tempus nunc est senem hunc adloqui mihi. 25
Hoc habet! repperi, qui senem ducerem,
Quo dolo a me dolorem procul pellerem.
Accedam. Di te ament plurumum, Simo.
SI. Salvos sis, Tranio. *TR.* Vt vales? *SI.* Non male.
Quid agis? *TR.* Hominem optumum teneo. *SI.*
    Amice facis, 30
Quom me laudas. *TR.* Decet certe. *SI.* [Certe] hercle;
    [at ego] te
Haud bonum teneo servom. [*TR.* Quid ita vero, Simo?]
TH. Heia, mastigia, ad me redi! *TR.* Iam istic ero.
SI. Quid nunc? quam mox? *TR.* Quid est? *SI.*
    Quod solet fieri.
TH. Dic [igitur, quod solet fieri,] quid id est. 35

[*SI.* Quid facitis vos? Sed ut verum, Tranio,] loquar,
Sic decet, [ut homines sunt,] ita morem geras;
Vita quam sit brevis, simul cogita. — Quid?
TR. Ehem, vix tandem percepi, super his rebus nostris
　　te loqui.
SI. Musice hercle agitis aetatem ita, ut vos decet :　　40
Vino et victu, piscatu probo, electili,
Vitam colitis.　*TR.* Imo vita antehac erat ;
Nunc nobis omnia haec exciderunt.
SI. Quidum?　*TR.* Ita oppido occidimus omnes, Simo.
SI. Non taces? Prospere vobis cuncta usque adhuc
　　processerunt.　　45
TR. Ita ut dicis, facta haud nego : nos
Profecto probe, ut voluimus, viximus ;
Sed, Simo, ita nunc ventus navem
Deseruit.　*SI.* Quid est? Quo modo?　*TR.* Pessumo.
SI. Quaene subducta erat tuto in terra?　　50
TR. Hei!　*SI.* Quid est?　*TR.* Me miserum! occidi!
　　SI. Qui?　*TR.* Quia
Venit navis, nostrae navi quae frangat ratem.
SI. Velim ut tu velles, Tranio. Sed quid est negoti?
　　TR. Eloquar.
Herus peregre venit.　*SI.* Tunc [tibi actutum] chor[da]
　　tenditur,
Inde ferriterium; postea —　[*TR.* Pol per tua te g]enua
　　opsecro　　55
Ne indicium hero facias meo.　*SI.* E me, ne quid met-
　　uas, nil sciet.

ACTVS III.   SCENA II.

TR. Patrone, salve.   *SI.* Nil moror mi istiusmodi
    cluentis.
TR. Nunc hoc, quod ad te noster me misit senex —
SI. Hoc mihi responde primum, quod ego te rogo:
Iam de istis rebus voster quid sensit senex?   60
TR. Nihil quicquam.   *SI.* Numquid increpavit filium?
TR. Tam liquidus est, quam liquida esse tempestas
    solet.
Nunc te hoc orare iussit opere maxumo,
Vt sibi liceret inspicere has aedis tuas.
SI. Non sunt venales.   *TR.* Scio equidem istuc; sed
    senex   65
Gunaeceum aedificare volt hic in suis,
Et balineas et ambulacrum et porticum.
SI. Quid [ille] consomniavit?   *TR.* Ego dicam tibi.
Dare volt uxorem filio, quantum potest:
Ad eam rem facere volt novom gunaeceum.   70
Nam sibi laudasse hasce ait architectonem
Nescio quem, esse aedificatas has sane bene:
Nunc hinc exemplum capere volt, nisi tu nevis.
SI. Nam ille ex malo [malum] hinc opere exemplum
    petit.
TR. Quin aestu aud[ivit] esse ibi vi[ctum] perbo-
    num: 75
Sub diu col[ere te] usque perpetuom diem.
SI. Imo edepol vero, quom usquequaque umbra est,
    tamen
Sol semper hic est usque a mani ad vesperum;

Quasi flagitator astat usque ad ostium ;
Nec mihi umbra usquam est, nisi si in puteo quaepiam
  est.   80
TR. Quid ? Sarsinatis ecqua est, si Vmbram non habes ?
SI. Molestus ne sis. Haec sunt sicut praedico.
TR. Attamen inspicere volt. *SI.* Inspiciat, si lubet.
Si quid erit, quod illi placeat, de exemplo meo
Ipse aedificato. *TR.* Eon' ? voco huc hominem ? *SI.*
  [I,] voca.   85
TR. Alexandrum magnum atque Agathoclem aiunt
  maxumas
Duo res gessisse : quid mihi fiet tertio,
Qui solus facio facinora inmortalia ?
Vehit hic clitellas, vehit hic autem alter senex.
Novitium mihi quaestum institui non malum ·   90
Nam muliones mulos clitellarios
Habent ; ego habeo homines clitellarios.
Magni sunt oneris ; quidquid inponas, vehunt.
Nunc hunc haud scio an conloquar. Congrediar.
Heus, Theuropides ! *TH.* Hem, quis hic nominat
  me ?   95
TR. Hero servos multimodis suo fidus. *TH.* Vnde is ?
TR. Quod me miseras, adfero omne impetratum.
TH. Quid illic, opsecro, tam diu restitisti ?
TR. Seni non erat otium : id sum opperitus.
TH. Antiquom optines hoc tuum, tardus ut sis.   100
TR. Heus tu, si voles verbum hoc cogitare,

Simul flare sorbereque haud factu facile est:
Ego hic esse et illi simul haud potui.
TH. Quid nunc? *TR.* Vise, specta, tuo usque arbi-
    tratu.
TH. Age, duc me. *TR.* Num moror? *TH.* Supsequor
    te. 105
TR. Senex ipsus te ante ostium, eccum, opperitur.
Sed [is] maestus est, se hasce vendidisse.
TH. Quid tandem? *TR.* Orat, ut suadeam Philolacheti,
Vt istas remittat sibi. *TH.* Haud opinor.
Sibi quisque ruri metit. Si male emptae 110
Forent, nobis has redhibere haud liceret.
Lucri quidquid est, id domum trahere oportet.
Misericordias [iam habere haud] hominem oportet.
TR. Morare hercle [quom verba] facis; supsequere.
    TH. Fiat.
TR. Do tibi ego operam. Senex illic est. — Hem, tibi
    adduxi hominem. 115
SI. Salvom te advenisse peregre gaudeo, Theuropides.
TH. Di te ament. *SI.* Inspicere hic aedis te has velle
    aiebat mihi.
TH. Nisi tibi incommodum est. *SI.* Imo commodum.
    I intro atque inspice.
TH. At enim mulieres. *SI.* Cave tu ullam flocci faxis
    mulierem.
Qualibet perambula aedis oppido tamquam tuas. 120
TH. Tamquam? *TR.* Ah, cave tu illi obiectes nunc
    in aegritudine,

Te has emisse. Non tu vides hunc, voltu ut tristi est
    senex?
TH. Video. *TR.* Ergo inridere ne videare et gestire
    admodum,
Noli facere mentionem, te [has] emisse. *TH.* Intellego,
Et bene monitum duco, atque te existumo humano in-
    genio.   125
Quid nunc? *SI.* Quin tu is intro? atque otiose per-
    specta, ut lubet.
TH. Bene benigneque arbitror te facere. *SI.* Factum
    edepol volo.
TR. Viden' vestibulum ante aedis hoc et ambulacrum,
    quoiusmodi?
TH. Luculentum edepol profecto! *TR.* Age, specta,
    postes quoiusmodi,
Quanta firmitate facti, et quanta crassitudine!   130
TH. Non videor vidisse postis pulcriores. *SI.* Pol
    mihi
Eo pretio empti fuerant olim. *TR.* Audin' 'fuerant'
    dicere?
Vix videtur continere lacrumas. *TH.* Quanti hosce
    emeras?
SI. Tris minas pro istis duobus praeter vecturam dedi.
TH. Hercle quin multum inprobiores sunt, quam a
    primo credidi.   135
TR. Quapropter? *TH.* Quia edepol ambo ab infumo
    tarmes secat.
TR. Intempestivos excisos credo; id eis vitium nocet.

ACTVS III. SCENA II.

Atque etiam nunc satis boni sunt, si sunt inducti pice.
Non enim haec pultiphagus opifex opera fecit barbarus.
Viden' coagmenta in foribus? *TH.* Video. *TR.*
    Specta, quam arte dormiunt.   140
TH. Dormiunt? *TR.* Illud quidem, ut conivent, volui
    dicere.
Satin' habes? *TH.* Vt quicquid magis contemplor,
    tanto magis placet.
TR. Viden' pictum, ubi ludificatur cornix una volturios
    duos?
TH. Non edepol video. *TR.* At ego video [eam inter]
    volturios duos;
Cornix astat; ea volturios duos vicissim vellicat.   145
Quaeso, huc ad me specta, cornicem ut conspicere pos-
    sies.
Iam vides? *TH.* Profecto nullam equidem illic corni-
    cem intuor.
TR. At tu isto ad vos optuere, quoniam cornicem
    nequis
Conspicari, si volturios forte possis contui.
Iam vides? *TH.* Non edepol video. *TR.* At ego vol-
    turios duos.   150
TH. Omnino, ut te apsolvam, nullam pictam conspicio
    hic avem.
TR. Age, iam mitto. Ignosco: aetate non quis op-
    tuerier.
TH. Haec, quae possum, ea mihi profecto cuncta vehe-
    menter placent.

SI. Latius demum est operae pretium ivisse. *TH.*
   Recte edepol mones.
SI. Eho, istum, puer, circumduce has aedis et concla-
   via.   155
Nam egomet ductarem, nisi mi esset ad forum negotium.
TH. Apage istum [circumductorem]: nihil moror duc-
   tarier.
Quidquid est, [errabo potius, quam] perductet quispiam.
SI. Aedis dico.   *TH.* Ergo intro eo sine perductore?
   SI. I, licet.
TH. Ibo intro igitur.   *TR.* Mane, sis: videam, ne
   canis— *TH.* Agedum, vide.   160
TR. Est. Abi. Canis est. Abi dierecta! St! Abin'
   hinc, in malam crucem?
At etiam restas? St! abi istinc! *SI.* Nihil pericli
   est. Age.
Tam placida est, quam est aqua, vise: ire intro audacter
   licet.
Eo ego hinc ad forum.   *TH.* Fecisti commode. Bene
   ambula.—
Tranio, age, canem istam a foribùs [aliquis] abducat
   face,   165
Etsi non metuenda est.   *TR.* Quin tu illam aspice, ut
   placide accubat!
Nisi molestum vis videri te atque ignavom— *TH.*
   Iam, ut lubet.
TR. Sequere hac me igitur. *TH.* Equidem haud usquam
   a pedibus apscedam tuis.

ACTVS IV. SCENA I.

Phaniscvs.

Servi qui, quom culpa carint, tamen malum metuont,
Hi solent esse heris utibiles.
Nam illi, qui nihil metuont, postquam sunt malum mer-
  iti,
Stulta sibi expetunt consilia.
Exercent sese ad cursuram: fugiunt. Sed hi si repre-
  hensi sunt,   5
Faciunt a malo peculium quod nequeunt [a bono].
Augent ex pauxillo; [thesaurum in]de parant.
Mihi in pectore consili [quod est, lubet cavere] malam
  rem prius
Quam ut meum [tergum doleat].
Vt adhuc fuit mihi, corium esse oportet,   10
Sincerum, atque ut votem verberari.
Si huic imperabo, probe tectum habebo.
Malum quom inpluit ceteros, ne inpluat mihi.
Nam ut servi volunt esse herum, ita solet.
Boni sunt, [bonus est]; improbi sunt, malus fit.   15
Nam nunc domi nostrae tot pessumi vivont,
Peculi sui prodigi, plagigeruli: ubi advorsum ut eant
Vocantur hero — 'Non eo, molestus ne sis,
Scio quo properas, gestis aliquo iam hercle, ire vis, mula,
  foras pastum.'

Bene merens hoc pretium inde apstuli: abii foras : 20
Solus nunc eo advorsum hero ex plurumis servis.
Hoc die crastini quom herus resciverit,
Mani castigabit eos bubulis exuviis.
Postremo minoris pendo tergum illorum quam meum ;
Illi erunt bucaedae multo potius quam ego sim restio. 25

Phaniscvs. Servos Alivs.

SE. Mane tu atque adsiste ilico,
Phanisce, etiam respice. *PH.* Mihi molestus ne sis.
SE. Vide ut fastidit simia. *PH.* Mihi sum : lubet esse:
    quid id curas ?
SE. Manesne ilico, inpure parasite ?
PH. Qui parasitus sum ? *SE.* Ego enim dicam ; cibo
    perduci poteris quovis ; 30
Ferocem facis quia te herus tam amat. *PH.* Vah,
Oculi dolent. *SE.* Cur ? *PH.* Quia fumus molestus.
SE. Tace, sis, faber qui cudere soles plumbeos numos.
PH. Non potes tu cogere me ut tibi maledicam;
Novit herus me. *SE.* Suam quidem pol culcitullam
    oportet. 35
PH. Si sobrius sis, male non dicas. *SE.* Tibi optem-
    perem, quom tu mihi nequeas!
PH. At tu mecum, pessume, i advorsus. *SE.* Quaeso
    hercle, apstine
Iam sermonem de istis rebus. *PH.* Faciam, et pultabo
    fores.

Heus! ecquis hic est, maxumam qui his iniuriam
Foribus defendat? ecquis, ecquis huc exit atque aperit? 40
Nemo hinc quidem foras exit: ut esse addecet nequam
    homines, ita sunt:
Sed eo magis cauto est opus, ne huc exeat, qui male me
    mulcet.

ACTVS IV. SCENA II.

Tranio. Thevropides.

TR. Quid tibi visum est mercimoni? *TH.* Totus
    gaudeo.
TR. Num nimio emptae tibi videntur? *TH.* Numquam
    edepol ego me scio
Vidisse umquam abiectas aedes, nisi modo hasce. *TR.*
    Ecquid placent?
TH. Ecquid placeant, me rogas? Imo hercle vero per-
    placent.
TR. Quoiusmodi gunaeceum? quid porticum? *TH.*
    Insanum bonam. 5
Non equidem ullam in publico esse maiorem hac exis-
    tumo.
TR. Quin ego ipse et Philolaches in publico omnis por-
    ticus
Sumus commensi. *TH.* Quid igitur? *TR.* Longe om-
    nium longissuma est.

TH. Di immortales, mercimoni lepidi! [Si] hercle nunc ferat
Sex talenta magna argenti pro istis praesentaria, 10
Numquam accipiam. *TR.* Si hercle accipere cupias, ego numquam sinam.
TH. Bene res nostra conlocata est istoc mercimonio.
TR. Me suasore atque inpulsore id factum audacter dicito,
Qui subegi, faenore argentum ab danista ut sumeret,
Quod isti dedimus arraboni. *TH.* Servavasti omnem ratem. 15
Nempe octoginta debentur huic minae? *TR.* Haud numo amplius.
TH. Hodie accipiat. *TR.* Ita enimvero, ne qua causa supsiet,
Vel mihi denumerato; ego illi porro denumeravero.
TH. At enim ne quid captioni mihi sit, si dederim tibi.
TR. Egone te ioculo modo ausim dicto aut facto fallere? 20
TH. Egon' aps te ausim non cavere, ne quid committam tibi?
TR. Quia tibi umquam quicquam, postquam tuus sum, verborum dedi?
TH. Ego enim cavi recte. *TR.* Eam [mihi] debes gratiam, atque animo meo.
TH. Sat sapio, si aps te modo uno caveo. *TR.* Tecum sentio.
TH. Nunc abi rus: dic, me advenisse, filio. *TR.* Faciam, ut voles. 25

TH. Curriculo iube in urbem veniat iam simul tecum.
TR. Licet.
Nunc ego me illac per posticum ad congerrones conferam :
Dicam, ut hic res sint quietae atque ut hunc hinc amoverim.

ACTVS IV. SCENA III.

Phaniscvs. Servos Alivs. Thevropides.

PH. Hic quidem neque convivarum sonitus itidem ut antehac fuit,
Neque tibicinam cantantem, neque alium quemquam audio.
TH. Quae illaec res est? quid illic homines quaerunt apud aedis meas?
Quid volunt? quid introspectant? *PH.* Pergam pultare ostium.
Heus, reclude, heus, Tranio! Etiamne aperis? *TH.* Quae haec est fabula? 5
PH. Etiamne aperis? Callidamati nostro advorsum venimus.
TH. Heus vos, pueri, quid istic agitis? quid istas aedis frangitis?
PH. Herus hic noster potat. *TH.* Herus hic voster potat? *PH.* Ita loquor.

TH. Puere, nimium delicatus es. *PH.* Ei advorsum
venimus.
TH. Quoi homini? *PH.* Hero nostro. Quaeso, quoties
dicundum est tibi. 10
TH. Puere, nemo hic habitat: nam te esse arbitror
puerum probrum.
PH. Non hic Philolaches adulescens habitat hisce in
aedibus?
SE. Hic senex cerebrosus est certe. *PH.* Erras per-
vorse, pater:
Nam nisi hinc hodie emigravit aut heri, certo scio
Hic habitare. *TH.* Quin sex menses iam hic nemo
habitat. *SE.* Somnias. 15
TH. Egone? *SE.* Tu. *TH.* Tu ne molestus. Sine
me cum puero loqui.
PH. Nemo habitat? Hem! *TH.* Ita. *PH.* Profecto:
nam heri et nudiustertius,
Quartus, quintus, sextus usque, postquam hinc peregre
eius pater
Abiit, numquam hic triduom unum desitum est potarier.
TH. Quid ais? *PH.* Triduom unum est haud inter-
missum hic esse et bibi, 20
Scorta duci, pergraecari, fidicinas, tibicinas
Ducere. *TH.* Quis istaec faciebat? *PH.* Philolaches.
TH. Qui Philolaches?
PH. Quoi patrem Theuropidem esse opinor. *TH.* Hei,
hei, occidi,
Si haec hic vera memorat. Pergam porro percontarier.

Ain' tu, istic potare solitum Philolachem istum, quisquis
     est,   25
Cum hero vostro? *PH.* Hic, inquam.   *TH.* Puere,
     praeter speciem stultus es ;
Vide, sis, ne forte ad merendam quopiam devorteris,
Atque ibi melius quam satis fuit, biberis. *PH.* Quid est?
TH. Ita dico : ne ad alias aedis perperam deveneris.
PH. Scio, qua me ire oportet, et, quo venerim, novi
     locum.   30
Philolaches hic habitat, quoius est pater Theuropides,
Qui, postquam pater ad mercatum abiit hinc, tibicinam
Liberavit. *TH.* Philolachesne ergo? *PH.* Ita: Phile-
     matium quidem.
TH. Quanti? *SE.* Triginta talentis. *PH.* Μὰ τὸν
     Ἀπόλλω, sed minis.
TH. Ain', minis triginta amicam destinasse Philo-
     lachem?   35
PH. Aio. *TH.* Atque eam manu emisisse? *PH.* Aio.
     TH. Et postquam eius hinc pater
Sit profectus peregre, perpotasse adsiduo
Tuo cum domino? *PH.* Aio. *TH.* Quid? is aedes
     emit hic proxumas?
PH. Non aio. *TH.* Quadraginta etiam dedit huic, quae
     essent pignori?
PH. Neque istud aio. *TH.* Hei, perdis! *PH.* Imo
     suum patrem illic perdidit.   40
TH. Vera cantas! Vana vellem! *PH.* Patris amicus
     videlicet.

TH. Heu, edepol patrem eum miserum praedicas! *PH.*
 Nihil hoc quidem est,
Triginta minae, prae quam alios dapsiles sumptus facit.
Perdidit patrem. Vnus istic servos est sacerrumus,
Tranio; is vel Herculi conterere quaestum possiet.   45
Edepol ne me eius patris misere miseret; qui quom
 istaec sciet
Facta ita, amburet misero ei corculum carbunculus.
TH. Si quidem istaec vera sunt. *PH.* Quid merear,
 quamobrem mentiar?
SE. Heus vos! ecquis aperit has? *PH.* Quid istas
 pultas, ubi nemo intus est?
Alio credo comissatum abisse: abeamus nunc iam.   50
TH. Puere, iamne abis? *PH.* Libertas paenula est ter-
 go tuo;
Mihi, nisi ut herum metuam et curem, nihil est, qui ter-
 gum tegam.

ACTVS IV. SCENA IV.

Thevropides. Simo.

TH. Perii hercle! quid opus est verbis? Vt verba
 audio,
Non equidem in Aeguptum hinc modo vectus fui,
Sed etiam in terras solas orasque ultumas
Sum circumvectus: ita, ubi nunc sim, nescio.

ACTVS IV. SCENA IV. 53

Verum iam scibo : nam eccum, unde aedis filius 5
Meus emit. Quid agis tu ? *SI.* A foro incedo do-
  mum.
TH. Num quid processit ad forum [tibi] hodie novi ?
SI. Etiam. *TH.* Quid tandem ? *SI.* Vidi efferri mor-
  tuom. *TH.* Hem,
Novom! *SI.* Vnum vidi mortuom efferri foras.
Modo eum vixisse aiebant. *TH.* Vae capiti tuo! 10
SI. Quid tu otiosus res novas requiritas ?
TH. Quia hodie adveni peregre. *SI.* Promisi foras
Ad cenam, ne me te vocare censeas.
TH. Haud postulo edepol. *SI.* Verum cras, nisi [quis]
  prius
Vocaverit me, vel apud te cenavero. 15
TH. Ne istuc quidem edepol postulo. Nisi quid magis
Es occupatus, operam mihi da. *SI.* Maxume.
TH. Minas quadraginta accepisti, quod sciam,
A Philolachete. *SI.* Numquam numum, quod sciam.
TH. Quid ? a Tranione servo ? *SI.* Multo [hercle] id
  minus. 20
TH. Quas arraboni tibi dedit ? *SI.* Quid somnias ?
TH. Egone ? At quidem tu, qui istoc te speras modo
Potesse dissimulando infectum hoc reddere.
SI. Quid autem ? *TH.* Quod me apsente [tecum] hic
  filius
Negoti gessit. *SI.* Mecum ut ille hic gesserit, 25
Dum tu hinc abes, negoti ? quidnam, aut quo die ?
TH. Minas tibi octoginta argenti debeo.

SI. Non mihi quidem hercle; verum, si debes, cedo.
Fides servanda est.   Ne ire infitias postules.
TH. Profecto non negabo debere, et dabo. 30
Tu cave, quadraginta accepisse hinc ne neges.
SI. Quaeso edepol, huc me aspecta et responde mihi.
Te velle uxorem aiebat tuo gnato dare :
Ideo aedificare hic velle aiebat in tuis.
TH. Hic aedificare volui ?   *SI.* Sic dixit mihi. 35
TH. Hei mihi, disperii! vocis non habeo satis!
Vicini, perii, interii!   *SI.* Numquid Tranio
Turbavit ?   *TH.* Imo exturbavit omnia.
Te ludificatus est et me hodie indignis modis.
SI. Quid tu ais ?   *TH.* Haec res sic est, ut narro
   tibi : 40
Deludificatus est me hodie in perpetuom modum.
Nunc te opsecro, ut me bene iuves, operamque des.
SI. Quid vis ?   *TH.* I mecum [hac] opsecro [te] una
   simul.
SI. Fiat.   *TH.* Servorumque operam et lora mihi cedo.
SI. Sume.   *TH.* Eademque opera haec tibi narra-
   vero, 45
Quis me exemplis hodie eludificatus [est].

ACTVS V. SCENA I.

TRANIO.

Qui homo timidus erit in rebus dubiis, nauci non erit ;
Atque equidem, quid id esse dicam verbum, nauci, nescio.
Nam herus me postquam rus misit, ut filium suum accerserem :
Abii illa per angiportum ad hortum nostrum clanculum.
Ostium quod in angiportu est horti patefeci fores ; 5
Eaque eduxi omnem legionem, et maris et feminas.
Postquam ex opsidione in tutum eduxi manuplares meos :
Capio consilium, ut senatum congerronum convocem;
Quem quom convocavi, atque illi me ex senatu segregant.
Vbi egomet video vorti rem in meo foro, quantum potest, 10
Facio idem, quod plurumi alii, quibus res timida aut turbida est :
Pergunt turbare usque, ut ne quid possit conquiescere.
Nam scio equidem, nullo pacto iam esse posse clam senem.
Sed quid hoc est, quod foris concrepuit proxuma vicinia ?
Herus meus hic quidem est. Gustare ego eius sermonem volo. 15

ACTVS V. SCENA II.

Thevropides. Tranio.

TH. Ilico intra limen astate illic : ut, quom extemplo vocem,
Continuo exiliatis.   Manicas celeriter conectite.
Ego illum ante aedis praestolabor ludificatorem meum,
Quoius ego hodie ludificabor corium, si vivo, probe.
TR. Res palam est. Nunc te videre melius est, quid agas, Tranio. 5
TH. Docte atque astute mihi captandum est cum illo, ubi huc advenerit.
Non ego illi extemplo hamum ostendam : sensim mittam lineam ;
Dissimulabo me horum quicquam scire. *TR.* O mortalem malum !
Alter hoc Athenis nemo doctior dici potest.
Verba illi non magis dare hodie quisquam, quam lapidi, potest. 10
Adgrediar hominem ; appellabo.   *TH.* Nunc ego ille huc veniat velim.
TR. Si quidem pol me quaeris, adsum praesens praesenti tibi.
TH. Euge, Tranio, quid agitur ?   *TR.* Veniunt ruri rustici ;
Philolaches iam hic aderit.   *TH.* Edepol mihi opportune advenit.

ACTVS V. SCENA II.

Nostrum ego hunc vicinum opinor esse hominem auda-
cem et malum. 15
TR. Quidum? *TH.* Qui negat novisse vos. *TR.* Ne-
gat? *TH.* Nec vos sibi
Numum umquam argenti dedisse. *TR.* Abi, ludis me,
credo. Haud negat.
TH. Quid iam? *TR.* Scio, iocaris nunc tu: nam ille
quidem haud negat.
TH. Imo edepol negat profecto; neque se hasce aedis
Philolachi
Vendidisse. *TR.* Eho, an negavit, sibi datum argentum,
opsecro? 20
TH. Quin iusiurandum pollicitus est dare se, si vellem,
mihi,
Neque se hasce aedis vendidisse, neque sibi argentum
datum esse.
Dixi ego istuc idem illi. *TR.* Quid ait? *TH.* Servos
pollicitus est dare
Suos mihi omnes quaestioni. *TR.* Nugas! numquam
edepol dabit.
TH. Dat profecto. *TR.* Quin et illum in ius iube ire.
TH. Iam mane: 25
Experiar, ut opinor; certum est mihi. *TR.* [Mihi] [huc]
hominem cedo!
TH. Quid, si igitur ego accersam homines? *TR.* Fac-
tum esse iam oportuit.
Vel hominem iube aedis mancupio poscere. *TH.* Imo
hoc primum volo:

Quaestioni accipere servos. *TR.* Faciundum edepol censeo.
Ego interim hanc aram occupabo. *TH.* Quid ita? *TR.* Nullam rem sapis : 30
Ne enim illi huc confugere possint, quaestioni quos dabit :
Hic ego tibi praesidebo, ne interbitat quaestio.
TH. Surge. *TR.* Minume. *TH.* Ne occupassis, opsecro, aram. *TR.* Cur? *TH.* Scies :
Quia enim id maxume volo, ut illi istoc confugiant. Sine :
Tanto apud iudicem hunc argenti condemnabo facilius. 35
TR. Quod agis, id agas. Quid tu porro vis serere negotium?
Nescis quam meticulosa res sit ire ad iudicem.
TH. Surgedum huc : est consulere igitur quiddam quod tecum volo.
TR. Sic tamen hinc consilium dedero : nimio plus sapio sedens.
Tum consilia firmiora sunt de divinis locis. 40
TH. Surge! ne nugare! aspicedum contra me! *TR.* Aspexi. *TH.* Vides?
TR. Video : huc si quis intercedat tertius, pereat fame.
TH. Quidum? *TR.* Quia nihil quaesti siet, mali hercle ambo sumus.
TH. Perii! *TR.* Quid tibi est? *TH.* Dedisti verba. *TR.* Qui tandem? *TH.* Probe
Med emunxti. *TR.* Vide, sis, satine recte : num mucci fluont? 45

TH. Imo etiam cerebrum quoque omnem e capite emunx-
   isti meo.
Nam omnia malefacta vostra reperi radicitus;
Non radicitus quidem hercle, verum etiam eradicitus.
Numquam edepol haec hodie inultus destinaveris.   Tibi
Iam iubebo ignem et sarmen, carnufex, circumdari.   50
TR. Ne faxis: nam elixus esse, quam assus, soleo suavior.
TH. Exempla edepol faciam ego in te.   *TR.* Quia placeo,
   exemplum expetis.
TH. Loquere: quoiusmodi reliqui, quom hinc abibam,
   filium?
TR. Cum pedibus, manibus, cum digitis, auribus, oculis,
   labris.
TH. Aliud te rogo.   *TR.* Aliud ergo nunc tibi re-
   spondeo.   55
Sed eccum tui gnati sodalem video huc incedere,
Callidamatem: illo praesente mecum agito, si quid voles.

ACTVS V. SCENA III.

CALLIDAMATES.   THEVROPIDES.   TRANIO.

CA. Vbi somnum sepelivi omnem, omnem atque obdor-
   mivi crapulam,
Philolaches venisse mihi suum [narravit] peregre huc
   patrem,

Quoque modo hominem ad[venientem] servos ludificatus sit;
Ait, se metuere in conspe[ctum illius] occedere.
Nunc ego de sodalitate solus sum orator datus, 5
Qui a patre eius conciliarem pacem. Atque eccum optume.
Iubeo te salvere, et, salvos quom advenis, Theuropides,
Peregre, gaudeo. Hic apud nos hodie cenes. Sic face.
TH. Callidamate, di te ament. De cena facio gratiam.
CA. Quin venis? *TR.* Promitte: ego ibo pro te, si tibi non lubet. 10
TH. Verbero, etiam inrides? *TR.* Quian' me pro te ire ad cenam autumo?
TH. Non enim ibis: ego ferare faxo, ut meruisti, in crucem.
CA. Age, mitte ista, ac ito ad me ad cenam. *TR.* Dic venturum; quid taces?
CA. Sed tu istuc quid confugisti in aram inscitissumus?
TR. Adveniens perterruit me. — Loquere nunc, quid fecerim. 15
Nunc utrisque disceptator, eccum, adest: age, disputa.
TH. Filium corrupisse aio te meum. *TR.* Ausculta modo.
Fateor peccavisse; amicam liberasse; apsente te
Faenori argentum sumpsisse; id esse apsumptum praedico.
Numquid aliud fecit, nisi quod summis gnati generibus? 20
TH. Hercle mihi tecum cavendum est: nimis qui es orator catus.

ACTVS V. SCENA III.

CA. Sine me dum istuc iudicare. Surge: ego isti adsedero.
TH. Maxume. Accipito hanc ad te litem. *TR.* Enim istic captio est.
Fac, ego ne metuam, [igitur, et] tu meam timeas vicem.
TH. Iam minoris [omnia fa]cio, prae quam quibus modis 25
Me ludificatus est. *TR.* Bene hercle factum, et factum gaudeo.
Sapere istac aetate oportet, qui sunt capite candido.
TH. Quid ego nunc faciam, si amicus Demipho aut Philonides —
TR. Dicito iis, quo pacto tuus te servos ludificaverit:
Optumas frustrationes dederis in comoediis. 30
CA. Tace parumper: sine vicissim me loqui. — Ausculta. *TH.* Licet.
CA. Omnium primum sodalem me esse scis gnato tuo.
Is adiit me: nam illum prodire pudet in conspectum tuum
Propter ea quae fecit, quom te scire scit. Nunc te opsecro,
Stultitiae adulescentiaeque eius ignoscas. Tuus est; 35
Scis, solere illanc aetatem tali ludo ludere;
Quidquid fecit, nobiscum una fecit; nos deliquimus:
Faenus, sortem, sumptumque omnem, qui amica [empta] est, omnia

Nos dabimus, nos conferemus, nostro sumptu, non tuo.
TH. Non potuit venire orator magis ad me inpetrabilis, 40
Quam tu: neque illi sum iratus, neque quicquam suscenseo;
Imo me praesente amato, bibito, facito quod lubet.
Si hoc pudet, fecisse sumptum, supplici habeo satis.
CA. Dispudet.   *TR.* Dat istam veniam. Quid me fiet nunc iam?
TH. Verberibus, lutum, caedere pendens!   *TR.* Tametsi pudet? 45
TH. Interimam hercle [te] ego, si vivo!   *CA.* Fac istam cunctam gratiam:
Tranioni remitte, quaeso, hanc noxiam causa mea.
TH. Aliud quidvis inpetrari a me facilius perferam,
Quam ut non ego istum pro suis factis pessumis pessum premam.
CA. Mitte, quaeso, istunc.   *TH.* Hem, viden', ut restat furcifer? 50
CA. Tranio, quiesce, si sapis.   *TH.* Tu quiesce hanc rem modo
Petere; ego illum verberibus, ut sit quietus, subegero.
CA. Nihil opus est profecto. Age iam, sine ted exorarier.
TH. Nolo ores.   *CA.* Quaeso hercle.   *TH.* Nolo, inquam, ores.   *CA.* Nequiquam nevis:
Hanc modo noxiam unam, quaeso, [missam] fac causa mea. 55

TR. Quid gravaris? Quasi non cras iam commeream
   aliam noxiam:
Ibi utrumque, et hoc et illud, poteris ulcisci probe.
CA. Sine te exorem. *TH.* Age, habe; abi inpune!
   Hem, huic habeto gratiam.
CANTOR. Spectatores, fabula haec est acta: vos plau-
   sum date.

NOTES.

The grammatical references are to Madvig, American edition (M.), Harkness (H.), Allen and Greenough (A. & G.), and Gildersleeve (G.).

ARGUMENT.

See Introduction to Mostellaria.

Manumisit is contrary to the custom of Pl., who commonly uses *manu emittere* (Lor.). *Manumittitis*, however, is found in Curc. IV. 2. 11.

Amores, "mistress," the plu. abstract for sing. concrete.

Apsente, apsumit, for *abs*—. See note on I. 1. 7.

Lucripeta. Formed after the analogy of the Plautine *lucrifuga*, Pseud. IV. 7. 33. On the composition see M. 205, *a*; A. & G. 168, *c*; H. 340; G. 790, II. *a*.

Ludus fit is not Plautine. In all the analogous phrases Pl. uses the plu.

Mutuom = *mutuum*. An imitation of the early form. See note on I. 1. 11.

Inspectat. The frequentative form for *inspicit*, in imitation of Pl. (Lor.).

PERSONS OF THE DRAMA.

The student will notice that the names are given in the order of entrance upon the stage in the course of the play, as in a Greek drama. Compare the arrangement in Shakspere according to rank or importance. See also Intro. to Most.

Servos. See note on *salvom*, I. 1. 11.

Pedisequi. See on II. 2, beginning of scene.

Advorsitor. From *advorsum* and *ire*, from the office of the slave, which was "to go to meet" his master after a banquet, and escort him home. Comp. *advorsum venire*, etc., I. 4. 1, where the custom is illustrated. The spelling *vo-* is invariable during the times of the Republic, in *voster* for later *vester*, and *vorto* for *verto*, with compound and derivative words.

Lorarii. These slaves appear frequently in Pl. Their office, as the name shows (*lorum*, a thong or lash), was to keep the household in order and to inflict punishment at the command of the master.

ACT I. SCENE I.

Grumio, a slave from the country, is before the house of Philolaches, calling to Tranio, who is busy within.

1. **Sis** = *si vis*. H. 293, 3; A. & G. 13, *c*; M. 157, obs. Translate not "if you please," but "come out, will you?"
1. **Foras.** An adv., but originally the acc. plu. of the obsolete *forae*, "openings," of which the adv. *foris* is abl. plu. *Foras* is an acc. of limit of motion, *foris*, abl. of place, or locative. The former therefore follows verbs of motion only, as here. (Ram.)
2. **Argutias**, "chaff," "quibbles," from stem ἀργ, shining. (Ram.)
3. **Herilis** takes the place of an objective gen., as in *custos herilis*, As. III. 3. 65, though generally for a possessive gen., as *herilis filius, res, patria*.
4. **Vlciscar.** This verb takes usually in Pl. and Ter. an acc. of person, as here, sometimes with abl. of manner. But also acc. of crime as in this play, third line from end, *utrumque ulcisci*. (Ram.)
4. **Probe,** "completely," "thoroughly," an ante-class. sense very common in Pl.
5. **Quid** = *cur*. So in next line, in 33, and very often in Pl. Perhaps originally an acc. of specification. G. 331, 3; H. 380, 2; 454, 2; A. & G. 240, *a*. Roby compares Gr. τί, but

suggests that *quid* may be the old abl. *qui* with *d paragogicum*. See II. 1. 18.

6. **Quid, malum,** "why the mischief," "why the deuce," Germ. "zum Henker." Very common in Pl. and Ter. Taken with *clamatio est*, the words may be rendered "why the mischief are you shouting?" This use of the verbal substantive is equivalent in some cases to the inf., as Poen. V. 2. 136, *acerba amatio est = acerbum est amare*, or to the gerundive, as Pseud. I. 2. 37, *cautio est mihi = cavendum est mihi*, or most frequently as here to the finite verb. So Trin. III. 2. 83, *quid tibi interpellatio est?* "why do you interfere?" Ter. Eun. IV. 4. 4, *quid huc tibi reditio est?* "why do you come back here?" (Lor. Wag. Hild.)

6. **Aedis** = *aedes*. The endings *-es* and *-is* for acc. plu. 3d decl. are both found in Pl. and are printed without distinction in this text. A third form in *-eis* is given in inscriptions. See M. 43, 2; H. 65; A. & G. 58; G. 60, 1.

7. **An** frequently introduces the second part of a disjunctive question, of which the first part may generally be supplied by the phrase, "Am I mistaken, or," etc. Such questions express the real or pretended surprise, incredulity or indignation of the speaker, when there is a contradiction between what would naturally be expected and what is evidently the case or is asserted to be the case. In this passage the full form would be, ("do you not know you are in the city, as you evidently are), or do you suppose that you are in the country, (as your shouting would lead any one to think)?" Render, "You think you are in the country, don't you?" So in II. 2. 24, *Eho, an tu tetigisti has aedis ?* "You have n't touched this house, have you?" "(Have you let this haunted house alone, as any one might expect you would) or have you touched it (as your words evidently indicate)?" So V. 2. 20. Less commonly in dialogue *an* expresses doubt inclining to one side or the other, as in I. 4. 20, *an scis?* "I don't think you know, do you?" These questions are especially fre-

quent in Pl. and Ter., and are often strengthened by *eho, opsecro, quaeso*.

7. **Apscede** = *abscede*. This early spelling is well established from inscriptions. Comp. note on *aps*, III. 1. 118.
8. **Abi dierecte**, "go and be hanged." The meaning of *dierecte* is evident from many passages in Pl., but the etymol. has occasioned much discussion. The most plausible derivation is that suggested by Rost and adopted by Ram. and Lor., from *dis+erigo*, referring to the position of the criminal, raised up (*erigo*) and spread out (*dis*) upon the cross.
9. **En.** With the word Tran. gives him a blow. "There! was it *this* that you wanted?"
9. **Hocine.** *Hoc* with the *e* which followed those cases of *hic* which end in *c*, shortened to *i* when the interrog. suffix *ne* is appended. "Less correctly," *hoccine*. M. 81, obs.; G. 102, Rem. 1; H. 186, 2; A. & G. 101, note.
9. **Perii**, a common exclamation of pain or fear. Perf. for pres. tense. See I. 3. 54.

Many of the differences between the language of Pl. and Ter., and that of classical prose, may be traced to one cause, viz. the desire for the most vivid and forcible expression. This appears in the use

(a.) Of the fut. perf. for the fut., of the perf. for the pres. and the plup. for perf. definite. (See I. 3. 54.)
(b.) Of pres. for fut. (See III. 2. 85.)
(c.) Of fut. indic. for impv. (See II. 2. 94.)
(d.) Of frequentative for simple verbs. (See I. 1. 51.)
(e.) Of synonymous words, particularly adverbs. (See I. 2. 17.)

To the same cause may probably be referred the use

(f.) Of *fui, fueram, fuero* for *sum, eram, ero*, with the perf. pass. participle. (See III. 2. 5.)
(g.) Of indic. for subjunc. in indirect questions. (See I. 2. 64.)

These peculiarities of style are not confined to comedy, but only show themselves most prominently there. Usages corresponding to several may be observed in English conversational style.

ACT I. SCENE I. 69

10. **Quia tu vis.** "Because by waiting about the house you invite me to strike you."
10. **Sine adveniat,** sc. *ut.* In the next line *sine* is followed by the inf. Such variations of expression are common in the conversational Latin of comedy. Notice also the omission of the subject of the inf., which is very frequent and almost peculiar to comedy. See M. 401, obs. 2.
11. **Salvom** = *salvum.* "Down to B. C. 100, or even later, the combination *vv* (*uu*) was unknown, whether the first *v* had the force of a vowel or of a consonant." (Ram.) Thus the earlier spelling was *volnus, volgus, servos, mortuos, quom.* In this text, however, the ordinary spelling *tuus, suus,* is retained.
12. **Frutex,** "you stick." So Ter. uses *caudex* and *stipes,* Heaut. V. I. 4.
13. **Vt possiet** = *ut possit.* M. 108, obs. 4; H. 204, 2; A. & G. 119, end; G. 191, 6. After *optimum est, aequum est* and similar phrases, *ut* with subjunc. is used when the truth or falsity of the occurrence is implied; otherwise, an inf. is used. See M. 374, obs. 2; H. 556, I. 2; A. & G. 332, *a*; G. 559.
14. **Scurra,** "dandy, swell." An excellent description of the Roman dandy in the time of Pl. is given in Trin. I. 2. 162–174.
14. **Vero** is regularly put in the third place in the sentence. (Lor.) Often in the second. M. 437, obs.; A. & G. 156, *k*; H. 602, III.; G. 489.
14. **Deliciae popli,** "darling of society." *Popli* is syncopated from *populi,* and is found six times in Pl. Comp. *manuplares,* I. 3. 154.
15. **Rus mihi tu obiectas?** "Do you cast the country in my teeth?" Ram. quotes a Scotch phrase "to cast up a thing to any one," which is still nearer the Latin.
15. **Credo** is parenthetic, and the clause beginning with *quod* is dependent upon *obiectas,* to be supplied from line 15. These lines may be paraphrased thus: — "Do you reproach me with being a rustic? I think you talk about the country because you have a premonition that you are soon to be sent there yourself to become a countryman."

16. **Pistrinum.** One of the punishments inflicted upon refractory slaves was to transfer them from the *familia urbana*, where the labor was light, to the *familia rustica*, where they were employed in severe toil. The grinding-mill was often worked by such slaves loaded with irons.
16. **Tradier** = *tradi.* M. 115, *a* ; A. & G. 128, *e*, 4 ; H. 239, 6 ; G. 191, 2.
17. **Cis paucas tempestates,** "within a short time." *Cis* is used in this sense only by post-class. writers and by Pl. who always connects it with *pauci. Tempestas* in Pl. commonly means "bad weather," but in one other pass. beside this, "season, time."
18. **Genus,** appositive of the subj. of *augebis*, or as Lor. says, partitive appos. of *numerum.*
18. **Ferratile.** Found only in this place, and probably coined by Pl. with reference to the fetters which Tran. would wear. The sense is, "you will become a new kind of plant in the country, the iron-bearing variety."
20. **Optumum** = *optimum.* The form in *u* is almost universal in inscriptions of the time of the Republic, and is generally adopted in Pl. and Ter. for superlatives and a few similar words.
21. **Pergraecamini,** "play the Greek," or "be true Greeks." (Thornton's Pl.) Numerous examples might be given of the Roman contempt for the Greek race. Warner compares Twelfth Night, IV. 1, where the clown is called "foolish Greek." Notice that Pl. here forgets that the speaker and the whole play are Greek, and uses the word from the Roman stand-point.
22. **Amicas.** Plu. used in angry exaggeration, as if the act had been habitual.
23. **Pollucibiliter.** *Pollucere* is the word for making an offering to a god, used particularly of the rich feasts in honor of Hercules. So *pollucibilis* means "rich, dainty, fine."
24. **Haecine.** See note on 9.
24. **Peregre** means (1) "in the country," "abroad," (2) "from

ACT I. SCENE I. 71

abroad," (3) "to a foreign country," and examples of the three uses may be found in Pl. Here it is (3), "to a foreign land." In II. 1. 6 and 27 are instances of (2). (Ram.)

25. **Offendet**, "find." And. Lex. s. v. I. B.
26. **Existumas** = *existimas*, like *optumum*, line 20.
27. **Vt corrumpat**, in apposition with *officium*. Comp. *ut possiet*, 13.
28. **Quom... studet** (= *quum*. See I. 1. 11.) Clauses of cause often take the indic. in early writers, especially when *quum* may be rendered "inasmuch as" or "in that," in which cases the idea of cause is not prominent. M. 358, obs. 2; A. & G. 321; G. 567, 587, Rem. So I. 2. 64, *quom scio*, "inasmuch as I know."
29. **Adaeque** is used only in Pl., always with a negative (here *nemo*), and always with a comparative force. And as in Pl. a double comparative is often used, so *adaeque* is often joined with a compar. *Adaeque parcus* (= *parcior*) corresponds therefore to *magis continens* (= *continentior*), and *quo* is abl. after compar. So Cas. III. 5. 45, *neque fuit me quisquam adaeque miser* (= *miserior*), "more wretched than I." Capt. IV. 2. 48, *adaeque nemo vivit fortunatior*, "more fortunate," double compar.
31. Notice the alliterative use of *p*, as of *c* (*qu*) in 52, below.
32. **Virtute** has here no moral force. Render, "power, force, influence." So Pseud. II. 1. 6, *malorum meorum... virtute*, "by the force of my evil deeds." So also in this play, I. 3. 17, *virtute formae*, "by the power of beauty." (Gron. Lect. Plaut.)
32. **Magisterio**, "teaching."
33. **Me**, object of *curatio*, the verbal noun taking the same case as the verb. The indirect question *quid ego agam* is in the same construction. So Aul. III. 2. 9, *quid tibi nos tactio est?* "why do you touch me?" See H. 371, 7; G. 329, Rem. 2. See also note on line 6, above.
34. **An.** See note on I. 1. 7.
36. **Tergi**, objective gen. after *fiducia*. See M. 283, obs. 3. "The

objective genitive with a substantive corresponds but very rarely with the dative governed by a verb." It is, however, quite common after *fiducia* (*fido*). See And. Lex. for examples. Render, "At the risk of *my* back," and comp. Bacch. IV. 4, 100, *mea fiducia . . . et meo periculo*.

38. **Allium.** See M. 223, *c*, obs. 2; A. & G. 237, *c*; G. 329, Rem. 1; H. 371, 3, 2). *Olere* is used transitively "by a stretch of the conception." (Roby.)

39. **Germana,** "pure, simple."

40. **Canes,** another and older form for *canis*.

41. **Olere.** This form must be of the 3d conj., as also *olant*, Poen. l. 2. 56, though *oles* in the next line is of the 2d conj.

41. **Unguenta exotica.** On the attempt to fix the date of the play by these words, see Introduction. The construction is the same as that of *allium*, 38.

42. **Superior ... accumbere.** Slaves and parasites sat on a bench at the foot of the table. To be placed on a couch above the host would be an honor given only to guests.

43. **Facetis.** This word in Pl. never means "jocose." In accordance with its derivation from *facio*, it means "apt, clever," and so "fine, graceful, dainty." In this line *vivere* must be supplied from *vivis*, depending upon *possunt*. (Ram.)

44. **Turtures,** etc. Greek dainties. Pl. in many other passages shows that pork in some shape was the choice Roman dish of his time.

45. **Alliato.** The text and construction of this line are doubtful. If *alliato* is the reading, it is abl. of manner. *Me* is then subject, and *fortunas* object of *fungi*, which like *utor, fruor,* etc. sometimes in early writers takes an acc. H. 419, 4, 1); G. 405, Rem. 1; A. & G. 249, *b*; M. 265, obs. 2. *Alliato* is found only in this place.

46. **Patiunda.** The form of the gerundive in *-und* is more common in early inscriptions than that in *-end*. It is confined to verbs of 3d and 4th conj., and verbs whose stem ends in *u* take *-end*. M. 114, obs., last clause.

47. **Maneat,** "await, wait for." The idea is, "I will endure my

present evil for the sake of the good which awaits me, while your evil is still to come."

48. **Quasi** is to be connected with *invidere.* "You seem, as it were, to envy."

49. **Dignissumum est.** "It is just as it ought to be."

51. **Victitare.** The frequentative for the simple verb is frequently used by Pl. So I. 2. 32, *mantant,* I. 2. 67, *victitabam,* and often. This is one manifestation of the tendency to exaggeration in popular speech, for vividness and force. See note on I. 1. 9.

51. **Pulcre** = *pulchre.* The early Romans used *h* very sparingly at the beginning of words, and did not aspirate consonants at all. So *triumpus, Kartago, teatrum, Pilolaces,* would probably be correct forms for the text of Pl. But editors are not agreed upon the limits of this general principle. (Ram. Lor. Rit.)

51. **Miseris modis,** "wretchedly." The use of *modus* in plu. with an adj. is very common in Pl. Comp. IV. 4. 39, *indignis modis,* "shamefully," Rud. III. 1. 1, *miris modis,* "wonderfully." Also I. 3. 35, *pessumis exemplis.*

52-54. In order to get the sense of these lines it is necessary to understand fully the mode of punishment alluded to. The *patibulum* was a beam or log with a hollow in one side, so that it could be laid across the neck and shoulders of the criminal: his hands were then bound or nailed to the projecting ends, and he was compelled to walk in this way to the place of execution without the walls. There the *crux,* an upright post, was permanently fixed in the ground; the *patibulum,* with the malefactor attached, was raised into position, and the feet were nailed to the *crux.* On the way the criminal was sometimes scourged, or driven with sharp goads which punctured the flesh. (Ram. Lor.) The latter custom explains the allusion in *cribrum. Carnuficium* is a conjectural form for *carnif-,* based upon *aurufex* for *aurifex,* which is found in one inscription. Before *fore* supply *te* as subj. *Patibulatum* is an adj. from *patibulum.*

53. **Ita.** "Instead of a consecutive sentence [clause of result] with *ut*, the consequence is sometimes stated absolutely in the indicative." (Roby.) This absolute use of *ita* is very common in Pl. The idea is, "You will be like a sieve, they will prick you so."

54. **Si ... quam primum,** "if once," or "as soon as." See also on I. 2. 17.

55. **Qui scis,** "how do you know." *Qui* is an old form of the abl. of *qui* or *quis*, and stands for any gender, and sometimes apparently for the plu. number.

  (a.) As relative, we have in this play, I. 3. 109, *lapidem, qui* (masc.), I. 3. 101, *cerussa, qui* (fem.), III. 1. 7, *argentum, qui* (neut.). In Stich. II. 1. 20, *quadrigas, qui* (plu.).

  (b.) As interrogative, *qui* is used either in direct or in indirect questions, with the meaning "how" or "why."

  (c.) As indefinite, *qui* is used for *aliquo*, or in compound *aliqui* for *aliquo*, in I. 3. 18.

The phrase *qui scis* is frequent in Hor. (Ram.)

55. **An.** See M. 453, foot of page. *Qui scis* is equiv. to *nescis*.

55. **Istuc** = *istud + ce*. M. 82, 3, obs. 2; A. & G. 101, *a*; H. 186, 3; G. 102, Rem. 2.

57. **Compendi face** = *compendii fac*. On form *face*, see M. 114, *c*, obs.; H. 237, 1; A. & G. 128, *c*. The expression *compendi facere*, "to save," is analogous to *lucri facere*, "to gain," and perhaps to *praemii, mercedis* or *dotis dare*. It is sometimes called the "predicative" genitive, and is placed by Roby under the general head of gen. of "kind or contents; that in or of which a thing consists." It is therefore like *acervus frumenti*, denoting indefinitely the sort or material of an object. This is not to be connected with *flocci* (*nauci*) *facere*. Comp. Bacch. II. 2. 6, *compendi ... verba ... faciam*, "I will save words," Pers. IV. 3. 2, *compendi feci binos panes indies*, "I have saved two loaves a day."

58. **Mactari,** "to be punished," the usual bad sense in Pl. See And. Lex.

59. **Daturin',** = *daturine*. M. 6, obs. 2; A. & G. 13, *c*. In next line with *estis* supply *daturi*.

61. **Quoniam,** as if in two words *quom iam,* as often in Pl. *Quom,* having the meaning "inasmuch as," takes the indic. as in 28. Render "Go on, now that you have begun." This is almost equiv. to the common Plautine phrase *ut occepisti, perge porro,* e. g., Trin. I. 2. 125.
62. **Saginam.** This word, which is found also in I. 3. 79, is somewhat difficult of explanation, and has been the occasion of much varying comment. And. Lex. translates this pass. (sub *sag.*) "Kill the fatted beast," but Ramsay's rendering is better in connection with *effercite vos,* "Stuff yourselves like sausages! chop up the meat for fattening yourselves!"
63. **In Piraeum.** Pl. is undecided in his construction of names of places, sometimes using a preposition, sometimes omitting it. (Lor.) The fish-market of Athens was at the Piraeus.
64. **In vesperum.** Comp. Eng. phrase, "against evening."
64. **Parare** depends upon *ire.* Later usage would require the supine, but the inf. is very common in Pl. after verbs of motion.
65. **Faxo.** "The future in *-so* is used as a completed future [fut. perf.] in subordinate relative sentences, or with adverbs of time or condition. *Faxo* only and in the first person only is also used as a simple future." (Roby.) This form is made by adding *-so* (*-sso* in 1st and 2d conj., *enicasso* I. 3. 55.) to the pres. stem. See M. 115, *f.* Taken by many to be shortened from fut. perf. *fecero,* through *feceso. Faxo* has two constructions in Pl. It is sometimes parenthetic, in which case the principal verb is usually in the fut., and sometimes, as here, it is followed by a subjunctive with *ut* understood. It is very common in Pl. and Ter., and is retained in later writers.
66. **Optuere** = *obtuere,* from collat form *obtuor* of 3d conj. Comp. *olere,* 41, *contui,* III. 2. 149, and *intuor,* III. 2. 147.
66. **Furcifer,** *furca* + *fero.* The *furca* was a V-shaped beam used in the same way as the *patibulum,* 52-54.
67. **Istuc nomen,** i. e., *furcifer.*
68. The sense is: — " Provided that I may in the mean time be in

as good condition as this, I am not disturbed about that which is to come soon."

69. **Nimio.** *Nimius* in all its forms, and the adv. *nimis*, have in Pl. beside the usual meaning "too much," "too great," a simple intensive force, "very great," "very." So here, in I. 3. 109, II. 2. 12, etc. In I. 3. 134, both meanings are found; in IV. 3. 9, either will suit. The context must determine which sense is required.

71. **Molestus ne sis** is a common answer in Pl. to an annoying joke. III. 1. 68, III. 2. 82, etc.

71. **Nunc iam.** Often written as one word. The pleonastic use of advs. is characteristic of conversation. See I. 2. 17.

72. **Praeterhac** is rendered "furthermore, moreover" by And. Lex. Perhaps better = *posthac*, "henceforward," as in several passages. *Ne tu erres*, "lest you should make a mistake (I will tell you)." Thornton's Pl. somewhat freely translates,

"'T is the last time, be sure, you e'er shall stay me."

73. **Satin'** = *satisne*. M. 6, obs. 2. A. & G. 13, *c*. This word has two quite distinct uses in Pl., which must be distinguished by the context. 1. A question of fact with the original meaning of *satis* prominent, as I. 3. 10, *satin' haec me vestis deceat*, "suits me well enough," "is becoming enough to me." 2. A question implying feeling of some sort, delight and wonder, or indignation as in this place. Render, "Is it possible that he has gone?" (Ram.)

73. **Flocci.** After a verb of estimating, *facere, aestimare*, that which denotes the indefinite value is regularly put in the gen. M. 294 and obs. 1; A. & G. 252, *b*; H. 402, III. 2. 3); G. 379. With *flocci* (*nauci*) *facere*, a negative is regularly (but not invariably) used. Roby refers this form to the locative. See Vol. II. Pref. pp. 57–61.

74. **Opsecro vostram fidem,** "I beg for your protection." This phrase was so commonly used in conversation that it became merely an ejaculation like the Eng. "Lord save us!" For examples see And. Lex. sub *fides*, II. B. 2.

78. **Paucorum,** "but few," "only a few."

ACT I. SCENE II. 77

78. **Mensum.** The more usual form is *mensium*, but see A. & G. 59; M. 44, 1, *a*; H. 65, 3, note 4.

78. **Relictae reliquiae.** The repetition of the same stem in successive words is called *figura etymologica;* it is found in many places in Pl., and is often carried to an extreme. Capt. II. 2. 108, *bonis benefit beneficium*, Aul. II. 2. 43, *facinus tuis factis facis.*

79. **Eccum.** Such forms as this, compounds of *ecce* with the acc. of the demons. pronouns, are frequent in the comic poets. *Ecce* itself contains a demons. suffix *-ce*, and seems in these compounds to have the force of an imperv. of the verb " to see." There are three kinds of construction with *eccum*, all found in this play.

(1.) *Eccum* is used entirely alone, like *ecce*. V. 3. 6, *atque eccum optume.*

(2.) With a name following in acc., III. 1. 29, *eccum Tranium.*

(3.) With a noun, but without influence upon the construction, as in this pass. where *filium* depends upon *video*, or in III. 1. 78, *pater eccum advenit.* This is perhaps the most common use. (Lor.)

For the double demons. in these words, comp. Eng. " this here," " that there," French *ceci, cela.*

ACT I. SCENE II.

There was no changing of scenery between the scenes, and therefore no pause. Grumio goes out toward the country, having seen Philolaches coming upon the stage from the other side.

The monologue which follows is the first *canticum*, and the arrangement of its metre has been the subject of much discussion and conjecture. The present text follows the MSS. in nearly every case, making no changes for supposed metrical reasons.

There are several *cantica* by young men on the subject of love, as in Trin. II. 1, Merc. I. 1, Cist. II. 1. This is pronounced by Lorenz the best and most interesting.

2. **Argumenta.** That which pierces and carries conviction, and therefore followed by *in* with acc. Contrast *in corde*, in next line.

4. **Volutavi**, the common frequentative form.
5. **Quoius** = *cujus*. M. 86, obs. 1; H. 187, 2; A. & G. 104, *b*.
6. **Arbitrarer**. Subjunctive of indirect quest. after *disputavi*.
9. **Ei rei**. Comp. 34. *Dativus commodi*. (Lor.)
10. **Haud**. This word has been sometimes written *haut* and *hau*, on the authority of Ritschl, Proleg. to Trin., pp 99-102. See also Lor.'s note. A full discussion of the forms is given by Ram. Proleg. pp. 43-45, where it is shown by reference to early inscriptions that these are probably late forms and were seldom or never employed in the time of Pl. This is true also of *quot, quit, aliut, set, at*, etc., for *quod, quid*, etc., and the spelling with *d* is followed throughout this text.
12. **Vera**, predicate after *esse*, which depends upon *vincam*, "I will prove." *Vosmet* is subject of *dicetis*, 14.
13. **Scio**. The very frequent use of *scio, credo, opsecro, amabo*, etc., is characteristic of conversational language.
13. **Proinde uti ... haud aliter**, for *proinde ut ... ita* or *haud aliter ... ac*. The usual prose would be *proinde ... ac*. (Lor.) See below, 17.
13. **Autumo**, lengthened from *aio*, as *negumo* from *nego*. Ante-class. and a favorite word with Pl.
16. **Simul** goes with *mecum*, as in IV. 4. 43, *mecum una simul*. (Lor.)
16. **Gnarures esse** = [*g*]*noscere*, with which it is connected in etymol. Found also in the Prol. to Poen. 47, but nowhere else before post-class. writers. Governs *hanc rem* as the verb would do. (Ram.)
17. **Quom extemplo** = *simul ac*. The pleonastic use of adverbs is one of the manifestations of the desire for vividness in dialogue. Comp. V. 2. 1, *ilico intra limen ... illic*, and *quom extemplo ... continuo, una mecum simul, nunc iam, igitur demum*. See general note on I. 1. 9.
18. **Examussim**, from *amussis*, a carpenter's level. Render "well constructed," "true to the line." (Ram.)
19. **Laudant**. The subject is general, to be supplied from *quisque*.
20. This line is very corrupt in the MSS., and the text is con-

ACT I. SCENE II. 79

jectural and doubtful. As it stands, supply *expetunt* from 19. " Each one seeks for himself a similar model, even at his own expense."

21. **Nequam** is probably an adverbial acc. with some fem. noun like *virtutem* understood. It is used by Pl. as an indeclinable adj. among words of bad meaning, as Asin. II. 2. 39, *malus nequamque*, and in contrast to *frugi*, Pseud. I. 5. 53. Render, "worthless," "good-for-nothing."

22. **Familia**, the household of slaves, who would be careless in their treatment of a house.

24. **Tempestas** has here its usual Plautine sense of "bad weather," not as in I. 1. 17.

25. **Tegulas imbricesque**, "tiles and gutters" (Ram.) or roofing-tiles and joint-tiles" (Smith's Dict. Antiq.). together equiv. to the whole roof. So Mil. Glor. II. 6. 24. *confregisti imbrices et tegulas*, "you have broken the roof."

26. **Reddere alias**, "to make them new," "to replace with others."

26. **Nevolt** = *nonvult*. H. 293. 3; M. 157, obs. The other forms with *non* occur in Pl., as *non vis*, I. 4. 23, *non velint*, III. 1. 146. *Ne* is the older form of the negative as seen in *neque*, *nemo*, *neuter*, *ne quidem*, etc.

27. **Perpluont**. The compounds of *pluo* are used five times by Pl., four of them in this play. *Pluo* is generally intrans. and so *perpluo*, "to let the rain through," as in this pass. and in Trin. II. 2. 41, *ne perpluant*, "lest they let the rain through." But *pluo* also takes an object of the thing rained down as *sanguinem pluere*, "to rain blood," and from this comes the trans. use of *perpluo* in I. 3. 8, *tempestas ... quam mihi Amor et Cupido in pectus perpluit meum*, "which Love rained through (poured through my covering of modesty) into my breast." Also *pluo* is usually impers., but *perpluo* in this sense is often personal. Comp. note on IV. 1. 13, for *inpluo*.

28. **Aer.** A somewhat doubtful conjecture of Cam. for *per* of MSS. Render, "mist, vapor."

28. **Operam** for *opus*, the trouble for the troublesome work. (Lor.)

29. **Nequior**, compar. of *nequam*, 21.
30. **Magna pars** with plu. verb. So *quisque* above, line 19. Comp. Capt. II. 1. 36, *maxuma pars . . . homines habent*.
31. **Moram**, etc., "allow this delay." "Affect delay" (Th.'s Pl.). Perfect tense of customary action, like gnomic aorist. M. 335, *b*, obs. 3; A. & G. 279, *c*.
31. **Numo** = *nummo*. The doubling of semi-vowels was contrary to the custom of the early writers, though the rule was not invariable. (Ram.) Render, "for a trifle." (Lor.)
32. **Id faciunt**, i. e., *sarciunt*.
32. **Donicum** = *donec*. The etym. is uncertain but *donique* is a form used in inscriptions as equiv. to *donec*. *Donicum* is used seven times by Pl.
33. **Ruont** = *ruunt*, as *perpluont* above. *Denuo*, "quasi *de novo*." (Hild.) See And. Lex.
34. **Etiam**. Two uses of *etiam* are prominent in this play, both derived from the orig. sense *et iam*, "even now." *Etiam* is often "still," "still further," "again." So in this pass. "still further." In II. 2. 43, *circumspice etiam*, "look around again." II. 2. 88, *etiamne astas?* "do you still stand near?" (Ram. Excurs. III.)

The second use is given under II. 1. 36.
34. **Aedificiis**. Comp. construction of *ei rei*, line 9, above.
36–63. These lines contain the application of the foregoing remarks, 17–33, and a constant comparison will assist toward a full understanding of the rest of the scene.
36. **Primumdum**. The use of *dum* as an enclitic is almost confined to comedy. It is the acc. of *dius* (*dies*), compressed from *dium* to *dum*, and therefore means "a while." (Wag.) *Dum* is appended to adverbs and to imperatives, and may always be rendered "now." II. 2. 20, *quidum*, "how now," *haud etiam dum*, "not even now," *necdum*, "nor now." To imperatives, III. 1. 139, *pultadum*, "knock now," V. 2. 41, *aspicedum*, "look now." (Ram. Excurs. II.)
36. **Liberum**. This form and the longer one of the next line are for metrical reasons used without distinction.

38. **In firmitatem,** "with a view to strength." (Ram.) So in the next line, "that they may be good both for use and for ornament to the people."
40. **Materiae** = *rei familiari,* family resources.
41. "Nor do they consider expense in this as expense at all." Thornton's Pl. translates,

    "Expence on this account, they count for nothing."

44-45. A reference to the Roman contubernium, a sort of military guardianship.
44. **Itum,** sc. *est.* Impersonal.
44. **Danunt.** Used again III. 1. 30, and several times by Pl., but not by Ter. A longer form for *dant.*
46. **Eatenus.** So the MSS., but the reading is very doubtful. Rit. and Lor. have *protenus,* and *eatenus,* if it is retained, must have that sense. "At once," "then."
47. **Igitur** denoted originally a sequence of time (then) and only in later usage a logical consequence (therefore.) It has usually the earlier sense in Pl. and is often joined with other adverbs of time, as here. So II. 1. 33, *igitur demum,* Trin. III. 3. 52, *tum igitur demum.* For similar pleonasms comp. *tum iam,* 45, and *hic iam,* 23, of this scene.
47. **Specimen cernitur,** "a proof is seen." Comp. Bacch. III. 2. 15, *specimen specitur, certamen cernitur.*
48. **Ad illud ... usque ... dum.** The Augustan prose usage would have required either *usque ... dum,* or *ad illud ... quum a fabris abirem.* (Lor.)
48. **Frugi.** See note on *cordi,* I. 4. 10. This word is often called an indeclin. adj., but it was originally a dat., and is found in several passages in Pl. with an adj. in agreement with it, e. g., Pseud. I. 5. 53, *ero frugi bonae.*
50. **Inmigravi.** "After I had moved into my own disposition," i. e., "had become my own master;" carrying out the figure of line 21.
51. **Oppido,** "entirely, completely." Used as an adv.; in answer to questions "precisely," "exactly so." Very common in Pl. as III. 1. 23, *perii oppido,* "I am utterly lost." So I. 3.

9. Ram. derives it from *ops* through a conjectural adj. *opidŭs* or *oppidus*, an etymol. preferable to the common one, for which see And. Lex. The word belongs entirely to familiar writing.

52. **Ignavia**, "dissipation." The orig. idea is laziness, and from that worthlessness of all kinds.

54. **Mi.** Dat. for abl. of separation. This dative, commonly a person, is used after compounds of *ab*, *de*, and *ex*, by a vivid conception of the act of deprivation as a wrong done to the person. It is therefore allied to the dat. of disadvantage. See the statement of this principle in A. & G. 229, and note. G. 344, Rem. 2; H. 385, 4.

54. **Virtutis modum**, i. e., manliness, which is the *modus*, the measure and standard of all goodness, *aurea mediocritas*. (Lamb.)

56. **Optigere** = *obtegere*, depending upon *negligens fui* = *neglexi*. (Lor.)

57-8. These lines are explained and applied in the following scene, 6-9.

57. **Pro imbre** = *tanquam imber*.

59. **Res**, etc., "fortune, credit, reputation, manliness, dignity."

60. **In usu.** Comp. *in usum*, 39. The sense is about the same, "in respect to use," and "for use." The same idea is expressed by the nom. in 29.

61. **Ita.** Used absolutely as in I. 1. 53, and often in comic writers.

62. **Quin**, "in order that it shall not fall." *Queat* depends upon *quin*.

62. **Perpetuae.** This word is used by Pl. always in its orig. sense, "uninterrupted," never "perpetual." So in III. 2. 76, *perpetuom diem*, "the whole day, without interruption." IV. 4. 41, *in perpetuom modum*, "in an uninterrupted fashion, without a pause." III. 1. 5, *perii in perpetuom modum*, "I am undone without anything to check my downward course." In the same sense, III. 1. 19, *perpetuo perierint*. In the present passage, therefore, render, "fall without anything to stop it," or somewhat freely, "completely." (Ram.)

ACT I. SCENE II. 83

64. **Vt sum ... fui.** See M. 356, obs. 3.; G. 469, Rem. 1; A. & G. 334, *d.* The indic. for the subjunc. in indirect questions is frequent in Pl. and Ter. It arose in conversational language from the tendency to emphasize the question for greater vividness and to make the leading verb parenthetic. Thus in many questions with *quaeso, opsecro, cedo,* the question may be either direct or indirect. So III. 1. 21, *dixtine, quaeso,* III. 1. 81, *vide num moratur.* But in many cases the question must be indirect, as in IV. 1. 19, *scio quo properas,* "I know whither you are hastening." In I. 3. 42, *rem vides, quae sim et quae fui ante,* the subjunc. and indic. are used together. Comp. also note on I. 1. 9. (E. Becker, De Syn. Interr. Obliq.)

65. **Erat,** sc. *quisquam.* Rit. supposes a line to have dropped out, which contained *quisquam.*

66. **Gumnastica.** The letter Y did not belong to the Roman alphabet, and before the time of Caesar it is represented in words from the Greek by *u*. (Ram.)

67. **Victitabam volupe.** This is the reading of the MSS., but it exactly contradicts the rest of the passage. The best explan. of the words as they stand is that of Lambinus, making *volupe* equiv. to *jucunde.* "I spent my time in athletic sports, and so was living happily and pleasantly." Acidalius supplies *haud,* and Ritschl supposes the omission of a line.

68. **Discipulinae.** The original form, afterward syncopated to *disciplina.* Comp. *vinculum vinclum, populus poplus.* Best taken with *aliis* as double dat. after *eram.* (Lor.)

69. **Optumi quique.** The plu. of *quisque* is not common instead of the sing., but is found with superlatives in Cic. and Liv. (Lor.)

70. **Nihili.** Gen. of indefinite value. G. 379; H. 402, III. 2. 3); A. & G. 252, *b. Nihili* is frequently used as an adj., as *homo nihili.* Pseud. IV. 7. 2; Cas. II. 3. 29; Mil. Glor. V. 16.

70. **Id** refers to the idea of the preceding words; "Now that I have lost my character, I have found how great is the loss."

84 NOTES.

This use of *id* with general reference to the subject in hand would hardly be allowed by Augustan prose usage, but is found frequently in Pl. as in Aul. prol. 10, Trin. II. 4. 4.

After this line Philolaches retires to the side or back of the stage, perhaps to one of the streets leading from the front to the rear, where he can be seen by the spectators, but not by the other actors.

ACT I. SCENE III.

Philematium and Scapha, her maid, come out from the house of Philolaches, the latter carrying a small casket or dressing-case.

On the violations of stage illusion in this scene, consult Introduction.

1. **Ecastor.** This oath is stated by A. Gellius to have been used only by women, as *Hercle* only by men, and the usage of Pl. supports this, except in a few instances, where the apparent contradiction is probably due to mistakes in the distribution of the dialogue. See And. Lex. where this statement is denied, and Ram. Excurs. XVII., where it is satisfactorily supported.
1. **Frigida.** The three baths were *sudatoria*, *tepidaria*, and *frigida*.
2. **Rear.** Lorenz calls the use of the present tense after *lavi* a violation of the sequence of tenses, but may it not be said that *esse defaecatam* is logically the leading verb, while *rear* is logically parenthetic and present in tense? The sense would then be, "when I have been better cleansed, I think."
3. **Horno**, adv., "this year." This line seems to have been a proverb, which Scapha quotes without much connection, from mere good spirits and gayety. Philem. sees no connection, and Sc. herself confesses that there is none. A similar pass. occurs in Merc. V. 2. 101, sqq. (Lor.) Thornton's Pl. refers to I Henry IV, Act I, Sc. II.
4. **Attinet**, etc. "What has that harvest to do with my bath?",
5. **Venus venusta**, "lovely goddess of love." Comp. *grates gratas, amoena amoenitate amoenus*, and similar examples of the *figura etymologica*. (Lor.)

ACT I. SCENE III. 85

5-9. Comp. the corresponding lines, 52-63, of the preceding scene.
6. **Haec illa,** "this is that storm," of which I was speaking a moment ago.
7. **Detexit.** The usual meaning is "to lay bare," with acc. of object uncovered. (See And. Lex.) Here "to strip off," with acc. of the thing taken off and dat. of person uncovered. On *mihi*, see note on I. 2. 54.
7. **Quam,** obj. of *perpluit*. See note on I. 2. 27.
9. **Haec** = *hae*, nom. plu. fem. H: 186, 4, 1; M. 81, obs. The form was originally *haece*. G. 102, Rem. 1.
10. **Contempla.** The active form is ante-class. So Pl. uses *opino, moro, proficisco* for the later deponents. (Lor.)
10. **Amabo.** A very frequent colloquial expression, which in full would be, "I will love you, if you will do what I ask." It is commonly used as a polite form of request, "please," or "if you please." So below, line 140, and often. Comp. Eng. phrase, sometimes used at the table, "I will thank you for," "I thank you for."
11. **Ocello,** diminutive of *oculus*. G. 785, 9, *b*; H. 315, 3; M. 182, *b*. "The apple of my eye."
13. **Vestis fartum,** "that which is within the dress," the woman herself.
14. **Lepida.** Notice the change of meaning. See And. Lex. s. v. I. and II.
14. **Scelesta.** This adj. is often used by Pl. without serious blame, as III. 1. 1, where impatience only is expressed. Ramsay renders this pass., "the cunning jade is very knowing." So "villain" and "rogue," II Henry IV, Act II, Sc. II.
16. **Quin** = *qui* (abl.) + *ne*, "how not," "why not." See Ramsay's Excurs. VIII. Some uses of this word in Pl. and Ter. are so peculiar as to require extended notice. They may be grouped under three heads:
   (a.) Exhortations, usually with impatience or anger, under the form of a question expecting a neg. answer, or of an imperative. Men. V. 7. 11, *quin me mittitis?* "why

don't you let me go?" Below, line 30, *quin mone*, "warn me, why don't you?" equiv. to the other form, *quin mones*. So in this pass., "look, why don't you?"

(b.) The ordinary prose use, as in I. 2. 62, II. 2. 5.

(c.) *Quin* introduces a qualification or explanation of a previous statement, often amounting to a contradiction. It may be translated "well, then," "why, I tell you," "but." Cas. II. 4. 6, illustrates both uses, *quin emittis me manu?* S. *Quin id volo.* "Why don't you free me?" S. "Why, I tell you, that is what I want to do." Trin. IV. 2. 87. *Lubet audire, nisi molestum est.* S. *Quin discupio dicere,* where *quin* corrects *molestum*. "(Disagreeable!) Why, on the contrary, I am eager to tell you." Comp. use of Fr. *mais*.

19. **Gratiis,** "for thanks" (and nothing more), i. e., "without pay." This form is commonly used by Pl. for the later contracted *gratis*. (Hild.)

22. **Pol.** This expletive was used by men and women alike.

23. **Inridere.** The use of the subject with this verb, while it is omitted with *culpari*, is somewhat awkward, but quite in accordance with the custom of Pl. and Ter., who often omit the subj. of an inf. where later prose would require it.

26. **Amarem.** *Oratio obliqua*, as is shown by the change of tense. If the quotation had been made by another person, it would have been *ita Philolaches istam* (or *illam*) *amaret,* but Philol. uses 1st pers. (See H. 533, 3, 2.)

27. **Istaec me,** sc. *ita amaret.* Philol. is angry because Sc. has sworn by his love for Philem. of which he needs no assurance, rather than by her love for him, which he would like to hear confirmed.

27. **Infecta ... facio,** "I make null and void," "I revoke." A favorite phrase with Pl., as Truc. IV. 2. 17, *facta infecta facere.*

32. **Illi morem ... geras.** *Morem gerere alicui* means to suit one's ways to those of another, and hence "to comply with," "to favor." Comp. below, 69. From this come the adj.

ACT I. SCENE III.   87

morigerus and verb *morigero*. So line 128, *mores emit*, "buys the favors." (Ram.)

33. **Inservire amantem.** *Inservire* takes the dat. in Ter. and in all later writers. It is used three times by Pl.; in this place, in line 59 of this scene and Poen. IV. 2. 105, all with the acc. So also *parcere, ignoscere, indulgere*, and a few other verbs which in later writers have the dat., are used by Pl. with the acc. (Lor.)

34. **Nam** frequently implies an ellipsis of the clause for which the reason is given. So here, "Oh Juppiter, (I invoke your aid) for," etc. So III. 2. 74, IV. 1. 16. In I. 4. 3, *nam* introduces a general explanation, "(I say this) for," etc. From this ellipsis comes the pron. *quisnam*. (Ram. Excurs. VI.) For similar use of *enim*, see III. 1. 20.

35. **Pessumis exemplis,** "after the worst patterns," i. e., "in the worst way." So very frequently in Pl. *hoc exemplo, ad hoc exemplum*, "in this way." Comp. *miseris modis*, I. 1. 51.

38. **Benevolentem,** a substantive, as usually in Pl. Comp. Capt. V. 1. 15, *benemerenti = benefactori*.

40. **Non spero.** *Non* goes with the verb understood. "I hope not." Comp. Gr. οὐκ ἔφη, Engl. "I do not think so," and *nego*, "I say no."

41. **Postremo,** "in short," "in fine."

42. **Dicta ... factis.** Comp. the frequent contrast in Dem. and Thuc. between ἔργον and λόγος.

42. **Quae sim ... quae fui.** For mood in indirect quest. see note on I. 2. 64, and comp. also Cist. I. 1. 59, *loquere ... et quid est ... et quid velis*, where the indic. and subjunc. are used together.

43. **Nihilo.** Abl. of degree of difference depending upon a compar., perhaps *minus*, implied by the clause *quam nunc tu*. Rit. supplies *setius*.

45. **Me** is repeated for emphasis and to bring it near the verb.

46. **Comprimor,** pass. with middle force. Render the line, "I scarcely restrain myself from flying at the eyes of that temptress," and comp. the similar expression in Ter. Eun. V. 2.

20, *vix me contineam, quin involem in capillum.* The orig. meaning of *stimulatrix* is "a woman who urges," but it is used here and below, 62, in a bad sense, "one who urges to evil." So *facinus,* orig. "a deed," commonly, "an evil deed."

47. The order is *censeo oportere me solam esse opsequentem illi soli.*

50. **Mihi nihil esse,** i. e., "that I have spent all my money for her sake," referring to the price paid for Philem.

51–66. Lorenz argues that these lines are a dittography of 29-50, by some later hand, because they repeat the ideas with but slight variation, as well as the unusual construction of *inservire* with acc. and the uncommon word *stimulatrix.*

52. **Curem.** Subjunc. of appeal in direct question, *opsecro* being parenthetic.

54. **Pro capite tuo,** "for you." The head as the supposed seat of life was used for the whole person. So Pseud. II. 4. 33, *hoc caput = ego;* and the phrase *vae capiti tuo,* "confound you," is frequent, as in IV. 4. 10. (Ram.)

54. **Perdiderit.** The use of the fut. perf. where the Engl. uses the simple fut. is frequent in all Latin, but especially so in Pl. and Ter. The speaker projects himself into the future, and looks back upon the present as past (perf.), the perf. definite as plup., and the fut. as fut. perf. So III. 1. 58, *abiero,* V. 3. 30, *dederis,* for simple fut. M. 340, obs. 4. So *perii* very frequently with present sense, as I. 1. 9; M. 335, *b.* In II. 2. 85, 91, *appellaveras, extimueras,* for perf. See general note I. 1. 9.

54. **Id ... tantum argenti,** "that large sum of money."

55. **Perii.** This use differs but little from that given above. The perf. tense is for the pres., and that pres. has a fut. sense. See A. & G. 307, *e,* and comp. also 276, *c.* So Amph. I. 1. 164, *perii, si me aspexerit.*

55. **Enicasso.** Old form of fut. from *enico (eneco).* Comp. note on *faxo,* I. 1. 65.

56. **Vitileua.** This is exactly the reading of one MS. and nearly

ACT I.　SCENE III.

that of two others, and may be retained in the text, though the word is found nowhere else.

58. **Minoris pendam.** "Consider him of less worth (than I do now)."

59. **Facito cogites**, sc. *ut* and comp. the epistolary phrase *fac (ut) valeas*. Render, "take care to consider."

59. **Inservibis** = *inservies*. The 4th decl. has in early writers a fut. in *-ibo*, and imperf. in *-ibam*, for *-iam* and *-iebam*. So *scibo*, IV. 4. 5.

60. **Aetatula.** On formation see M. 182, 1, *a*. *Querere* is fut. 2d sing.

61. **Anginam,** a disease of the throat (*fauces*).

63-4. "I ought to have the same mind now, when I have obtained the favor, as formerly, before," etc. *Gratum* is best taken as a substantive.

65. **Me.** Abl., frequent in Pl. after *esse, facere* and *fieri*. "May the gods do with me what they wish." So III. 1. 103, *quid eo argento factum?* "What has been done with that money?" So I. 4. 33, V. 3. 44. (Lor.)

66. **Liberasso denuo.** Fut. ind. like *enicasso*, 55. The sense is somewhat difficult, as Philem. is already free, but perhaps the best rendering is, "if I shall not free you over again," making Philol. in his eagerness vow to do an impossibility, in order to express his love.

67. **Acceptum,** "certain," "if you are well enough assured that," etc. And. Lex. s. v. 5.

69. **Capiundos crines.** A full discussion of this disputed phrase is given by Lorenz. His explan. is as follows. The *crines* were six braids or plaits in which the hair of a bride was arranged, and which matrons were allowed to wear. These were forbidden to the *meretrices*, who were further distinguished by the dark robe. *Capere crines* therefore means "to be a bride or a lawful wife." The lines may be paraphrased thus: If you are sure that he will continue to love and maintain you, you must follow your own course, grant favors to him only, and act as a wife would. On the gender

of *crines*, see And. Lex. The reference is to Roman customs.

70. **Exin**, "so." Generally used of time or space, but several times in Pl. correlative to *ut*.

72. **Vendundum est**, impers. "If there must be any selling." Notice that *veneo* (*venum-eo*) is used as the pass. of *vendo* (*venum-do*). A. & G. 136, *b*.

74. **Illis ... ceteris**, abl. Comp. *me*, 65. "How will it be with," etc. *Quid*, acc. of specification, not subj. of *futurum*.

75. This line is imperfect in the MSS., and is filled out by Rit.

76. **Mortuos**, pred. nom. On form see I. 1. 11.

77. **Exheredem** is either adj. or substant., and is followed either by abl. as here or by gen. Comp. abl. or gen. after *inanis*, M. 268, *b*, obs. 2. (Lor.) So *vacuus*, H. 399, 2 and 5, and see G. 389, Rem. 3.

78. **Ista ... res**, "that fortune of his," in contempt.

79. **Sagina**. "It is a clear case of stuffing." (Ram.) Others render, "it is a regular fattening-coop," but the former is preferable. See note on I. 1. 62.

80. **Certum est**, "I am determined." So very often in Pl. *Te* is abl. Render, "I am determined to try the experiment (to make a beginning) upon you, to see how thrifty I can be."

81. **His ... diebus**, "within these ten days." Limit of time. M. 276; H. 426, (3); A. & G. 256. Especially common with *hic*. G. 392, 4.

81. **Decem**. A general term like Germ. "acht Tage," French "quinze jours," Engl. "ten days or a fortnight." (Lor.)

82. **In illum** = *illi*, as in next line.

83. **Nec recte**. The oldest form of the negative was *ne* (see note on *nevolt*, I. 2. 26), of which *nec* was a stronger form without connective force. It is particularly frequent in the phrase *nec recte dicere* (*loqui*) = *maledicere*, where *nec* goes with *recte*. Comp. *negotium* = *nec-otium*, *nego* = *nec-aio*, *necopinans*. (Lor. Ram.)

84. **Vivo argento**, "pure silver," "native silver," as opposed to that worked by art. (Rost. Opusc. I. 133.) Comp. Virg. Aen. I. 167, *vivo sedilia saxo*.

ACT I. SCENE III. 91

86. **Vt videas** = *utinam videas*, denoting a wish. This use of *ut* belongs especially to prayers and curses, and perhaps arose from the ellipsis of some verb, as *precor, quaeso*.
86. **Probus**, as often in Pl., has no moral force. " I am a fine fellow." This is like the common use of *probe*, I. 1. 4
87. **Quae** agrees in gend. with the person spoken of, rather than with its grammatical anteced. *patronum*. So Ter. Andr. III. 5. 1, *scelus, qui*, "the rascal, who." Adelph. II. 3. 8, *caput, qui*. (Lor.)
87. **Causam diceret.** The patron was expected to defend the client in any lawsuit in which the latter might become involved. An account of such a case is given in Men. IV. 2.
90. This line is regarded as an interpolation from 67.
91. **Cedo.** Probably from the demonstrative *-ce* and stem *do*. It is used in colloquial language as an imperv. 2d sing. Plu. *cette*.
91. **Arculam.** A toilet-box, containing cosmetics, jewelry, mirror, etc. Such chests have been found at Praeneste. (Lor.)
92. **Siem** = *sim*. M. 108, obs. 4; A. & G. 119, end; G. 191, 6; H. 204, 2.
92. **Voluptas mea**, " my delight." The vocabulary of Pl. is very full in terms of endearment. (See Ram. Excurs.) Comp. Poen. I. 2. 152, sqq. *Mea voluptas! meae deliciae! mea vita! mea amoenitas! meus ocellus! meum labellum! meum suavium! meum mel! meum cor! mea colostra! meus molliculus caseus!*
93. **Mulier quae** = *quae mulier*. See M. 319; A. & G. 200, *b*; H. 445, 9; G. 618.
93. **Speculo ei usus.** M. 266; A. & G. 243, *e*; H. 419, V; G. 390.
94. **Speculo speculum.** "Who are yourself the best mirror for a mirror." Comp. " The glass of fashion."
96. **Peculi.** The property which a slave or minor held for his own was called *peculium*. Philol. means that he will give something to Sc. to be her own.
96. **Tibi** would naturally refer to Scapha, but the name of Philem. is unexpectedly added. This form of witticism, which consists in saying the opposite of that which would be expected,

is frequent in Pl., and is called by the older commentators παρὰ προσδοκίαν. Comp. V. 2. 10, IV. 4. 15.

97. **Viden'** is parenthetic. On the form see M. 6, obs. 2. Shortened from *videsne*, as *iuben'* = *iubesne*, *ain'* = *aisne*.

99. **Pote**, sc. *est* = *potest*. *Potis* is used in all genders and numbers, and the form *pote*, neut., is also common in Pl. Either form is used alone with *esse* understood.

99. **Quicquam** used pleonastically with *quid*, as in Ter. Andr. I. 1. 63, *nihil quicquam*.

101. **Cerussam**, white lead, which was employed by Roman ladies as a cosmetic.

101. **Quid**, acc. of specif. as in I. 3. 4. *Qui*, abl. of rel.

102. **Vna opera.** Originally "with one (and the same) effort," often "at the same time," and occasionally as here "with the same effort, and the same hope of success," i. e., "just as well." The full sense is "This attempt is just the same as the attempt to," etc. (Lor.)

102. **Postules.** This verb takes in Pl. a mild meaning "to want, desire, expect," and is often used as in this pass. to throw contempt upon the foolish or extravagant desires of another person. Render, "You may as well expect." (Ram.)

103. **Euge** = εὖγε. The use of this and numerous other Greek words in the language of comedy indicates a considerable acquaintance with the Greek of conversation on the part of a Roman audience.

104. **Purpurissum**, "rouge." It was made by boiling fine chalk in the dye obtained from the *murex*. (Ram.)

105. **Interpolare.** Originally used of renewing and smoothing out an old toga. Render, "to improve."

106. **Istanc** = *istam* + *ce*, the demons. particle. The forms *illic* and *istic* have all the cases except the gen. plu. M. 82, 3, obs. 2. Second person, "such an age as yours."

107. **Melinum**, sc. *pigmentum*, "powder." So called, because the best quality came from the island of Melos.

108. **Philem.** takes the mirror from Scapha, and upon seeing her

ACT I. SCENE III. 93

own image reflected in it, kisses it. The exclamation of Philol. is an exhibition of jealousy.

109. **Speculo.** Dat. of disadvantage. The mirror was of polished metal, either silver or a mixture of brass and tin.

109. **Caput.** This phrase was originally used of persons as Men. II. 2. 30, *illi homini diminuam caput*, and thence transferred in a comic sense to things.

111. **Vt,** "inasmuch as." I have not been able to find any other example in Pl. or Ter. of this use. See And. Lex. s. v. I. B. 3; G. 645, Rem. 4.

112. **Vsquam,** "in any way." Ter. Andr. II. 5. 9, *neque istic neque alibi tibi usquam erit in me mora;* a rare sense.

113. **Videor,** sc. *mihi,* "I do not think." So Cas. II. 3. 11, *ut videor,* "as I think." Epid. IV. 1. 11, *nam videor . . . me vidisse prius,* "for I think I have seen her before." Comp. ὡς φαίνομαι.

114. **Malae,** gen. depending on *mentem.* Without serious blame, like *scelesta,* I. 3. 14.

115. **Vnguendam,** sc. *me esse.* The prose usage would require the expression of the subject, but the comic poets often omit it. So I. 1. 52, *credo (te) fore,* and below, 121.

115. **Feceris.** A prohibition, since *minume* has the force of a negative. Either perf. subj. A. & G. 269, *a*; G. 266, or fut. perf. ind. M. 386.

120. **Iura,** from *ius, iuris,* "broth."

120. **Cocus** = *coquus.* C, which had the hard sound, is in many words interchanged with *qu (qv)* as an equivalent sound. So *cum, quum, cotidie, quotidie,* etc. *Relinquo* has *relictus,* and *coquo* has *coxi (cocsi).* The earliest form seems to have been *coquos,* and when *o* was changed to *u, qu* also changed to *c.* The forms in *quu* are much later. *Reliquos* has *qu* in all the early inscriptions, never *c.*

123. **Maxuma pars** has here the sing. verb, though in I. 2. 30, *magna pars* is used with plu. An illustration of the freedom of Pl. in syntax, like that noticed in 115.

123. **Adeo** introduces the sentence, "Indeed, besides," or "indeed,

what is more," etc. So also in III. 1. 96. (For full discussion of this difficult word see Ram. Excurs. I.)

123. **Vostrorum.** "The old genitive of the 1st and 2d persons was *mis, tis;* the latter is found in Plautus. [Trin. II. 2. 62.] This was replaced as possessive by the adjectives *meus, tuus;* and as objective by the gen. sing. neut. *mei* (of my being), *tui.*" In the plural, "as possessive genitives the adjectives *noster* and *vester* were used; as objective *nostri, vestri*, and rarely *nostrum, vestrum;* as partitive *nostrum, vestrum* and in the comic poets sometimes *nostrorum, nostrarum, vestrorum, vestrarum.*" (Roby.) The forms *nostrum, vestrum*, are perhaps contracted from *nostrorum*, etc. See also, M. 79, obs. 1, 297, *b*; H. 396, 1; G. 362 and Rem.; A. & G. 99, *b* and *c*, and comp. Aul. II. 4. 42, *uter vostrorum*, Poen. IV. 2. 39, *nostrorum nemo*.

124. **Anus** is best taken as an adj.

124. **Meruerunt,** "bought." A similar tirade against *dotales uxores* occurs in the Aul., and the allusion is probably to the Roman practice of marrying for the sake of the dowry; Lorenz, however, believes it to be Greek, on the ground that the police would not have allowed such an attack upon the Roman matrons.

126. **Quem,** sc. *curare oportet.* So also with *Philolachem* in next line. *Is*, however, is the subject of some such verb as *curabit*, to be supplied from the context.

127. **Placere.** We should expect *decere*, and Rit. has supposed a line to be lost here which explained the sense of *placere*. We may take it to include both meanings, "to please because it is becoming."

128. **Mores,** "favors;" comp. the sense of *morem*, I. 3. 32.

129. The meaning is, "What is the use of showing to him for your own pleasure (*ultro*) that which he did not care to keep, but gave to you?"

131. **Nuda,** "unadorned." So *nudi capilli*, Ov. Met. IV., 261. "Beauty unadorned is adorned the most."

132. **Si morata est male,** "if she is a woman of bad character." So I. 4. 8, *istoc modo moratus*.

ACT I. SCENE III.

133. **Caeno**, sometimes, but less correctly, spelled *coen-*.
134. **Nimis**. The two uses of this word, mentioned in I. 1. 69, are well illustrated here. *Nimis ornata*, "very well adorned;" *nimis diu*, "too long."
136. **Intro** is used after verbs of motion, "to a place within." The command is addressed to Scapha, who goes into the house carrying the *arcula*.
138. **Quod ... idem.** Impers. verbs sometimes take a neut. sing. pron. as subject. This is especially common in Pl. and Ter. and is occasionally extended to the use of the plu. or 1st pers. So V. 3. 43, *hoc pudet*, Ter. Adel. IV. 7. 36, *haec pudent*, Cas. V. 2. 3, *nunc pudeo*. (Lor.)
139. **Istuc verbum**, the sentiment of the whole line, and particularly *mea voluptas*.
140. Philem. pretends to take the words literally. The idea of the lines is this: "Is it cheap at twenty minae? I will sell it to you at half-price; give me ten." Philol. answers in the same vein: "Cast up the account. You have the ten now, for I have given thirty minae for your freedom, and you have given me a compliment worth twenty, so that you still owe me ten." But Philem., seeing what he is about to say, interrupts, and turns the conversation.
140. **Bene emptum**, "at a low price." So III. 2. 110, *male emptae*, "bought at a high price," Amph. I. 1. 132, *conducto male*. In these phrases the adv. takes the place of the abl. of price or gen. of indef. value.
141. **Rationem puta.** This phrase, "to cast up an account," is used by Pl. in Trin. II. 4. 15, Cas. III. 2. 25, and by Cic. in his letters. (Wag.) *Vel*, "just," "only."
142. **Triginta minas.** The price of a female slave varies in Pl. from 20 to 60 minae. The price of an able-bodied man is fixed at 20 minae, Capt. II. 2. 103, and in the same play a boy four years old is said to have been sold for 6 minae. (Ram.) The Attic mina was worth about $18. These sums probably represent the Roman prices of the time of Pl.

143. **Egone.** Notice the surprise and dissent expressed by *ne* appended to the pron. M. 451, *a*; H. 346, II. 1.
143. **Quin,** etc. Philol. is so much pleased with what he has done that he even desires to bear reproach for it.
144. **Locavi.** Comp. the Engl. phrase, "to place a loan."
145. **Quod,** "as to the fact that." M. 398, *b*, and obs. 2. Pl., however, uses the subjunc. in this construction.
145. **Operam ... ponere** corresponds to *locavi.* " To expend my labor."
148. **Haec.** When *gaudeo* takes an acc., it is either cognate in stem, or a neut. pron. in cognate acc.
149. **Prosus** is the reading of the best MSS. for *prorsus.* Rit. translates it, "*in posterum,*" "for the future."
150. Here occurs one of those drinking scenes so frequently introduced by Pl. Fuller descriptions are given in Stich. V. 4, and Pers. V. 1. The form of tables and couches and the manner of reclining are explained in the Dict. Antiq. *Accumbe* is the regular word of invitation, commonly preceded as here by *age. Puer* is often used of a slave, and especially of one who waits at the table. Comp. Fr. garçon. After the guests had reclined and water for the hands had been brought, the table was set in its place before them. The dice, *tali,* were for determining the *arbiter bibendi,* whom Pl. calls *dictator.* Though the garlands which were commonly distributed on such occasions are not mentioned here, they were probably brought out upon the stage. This scene takes place in the garden or in the *vestibulum* before the house of Philol.
151. **Vin'** = *visne* as *viden'* = *videsne,* 97.
153. **Oculus meus,** nom. for voc. as often in poetry. The words are addressed to Philem. The others are making their way slowly across the stage, and do not come within speaking distance for some lines.
154. **Manuplares.** The full form is *manupulares,* shortened in later writers to *manipl-* or *manipul-.* Comp. *populus, poplus.* The military metaphor is continued through the line.

ACT I. SCENE IV.

Callidamates and Delphium come along the street, followed by several slaves. Philol. and Philem. remain at the table awaiting their coming.

Throughout this scene the metres, the division of lines, and even the distribution of the dialogue among the characters, are extremely confused in the MSS. Those editors who make changes for metrical reasons have remodelled the scene in various ways, according to their theories.

1. **Advorsum venire.** Comp. note on *Advorsitor* in list of Personae.
2. **Temperi.** Sometimes spelled *tempori*, but the word is used nineteen times by Pl., and in all cases but one the best MSS. read *temperi*. (Wag.) This is the locative case of *tempus*.
2. **Tibi** refers to one of the slaves, perhaps to Phaniscus, who performs the office of *Advorsitor* in IV. 3.
3. **Illi** is the locative from *ille* for the more common *illic*, which is locative from nom. *illic* (*ille* + *ce*), like adv. *hic* from pron. *hic*. So V. 3. 22, *isti* for *istic*. Used pleonastically with *inde*, as in Ter. And. IV. 1. 14, *illic, ubi . . . est, ibi verentur.*
5. **Philolachetem.** Greek proper names are treated with some freedom by the comic writers, especially those ending in $-\eta s$, from which various forms are made according to the metre. Beside the two acc. forms here and above, the dat. is either *Philolachi* or *Philolacheti*, abl. *Philolache* or *Philolachete*. So Ter. has from nom. *Chremes* (-ηs) *Chremem* or *Chremetem*, *Chremi* (gen.) or *Chremetis*. (Lor.) See M. 45, 2, *e*.
6. **Vbi . . . accipiet,** used freely for *qui . . . accipiet.* "To the house of Philol., where he will," etc.
7. **Ma-ma-madere,** "t-t-tipsy." *Madeo* and *madidus* are used euphemistically to denote intoxication. There is special point in making Call. stumble over this particular word.
10. **Cordi.** Dat. of object for which, M. 249, n. 2; G. 350; H. 390. Or dat. of purpose, service, or end, A. & G. 233. For full discussion of this dat. see Roby, Vol. II. Pref. pp. 25-56.

The following are among the general characteristics there given: "This dat. is (1) a semi-abstract substantive, (2) in the singular number, (3) used predicatively, (4) and most frequently with *est*. It is not qualified (5) by any adjective except the simplest adjectives of quantity, nor (6) by a genitive or prepositional phrase." *Cordi* is found eight times in Pl. and may generally be rendered "dear." But here render, "if you want to do it."

11. **Duce** for *duc* is used several times by Pl. as *face*, *dice*, for *fac*, *dic*.
13. **Modo**, "only," from *modus* in the sense of a limit. (Ram. Excurs. V.)
13. **Accumbas**, the regular word for reclining at the table, as in I. 3. 150. "Take care that you do not recline in the street instead of at the table."
15. The latter part of this line is so confused in the MSS. that little can be made of it. As it stands, it indicates that Call. is still supporting himself by clinging to Delph., to whose body *hoc* refers. The construction is *sed sine et hoc cadere*.
17. This line is given by some editors to Call. A similar line occurs in Pseud. V. 1. 2, *an id voltis ut me hic iacentem aliquis tollat?*
18. **Madet homo.** This is said in an undertone, but is heard by Call., who expresses his indignation in the next question by appending *ne* to the pron. Comp. I. 3. 143.
19. Call. had fallen, perhaps after line 15, and in the next line, 20, Delph. lifts him up again.
22. **Imo** or *immo*. Authorities differ as to spelling, etymol. and meaning. Perhaps the best opinion is that which spells it (in authors later than Pl. and Ter.) *immo*, from *imus* (for *inimus*, superlative of *in*), meaning "at the bottom," "in the least." In Pl. and Ter. always neg. The uses of *imo* denote:—

(a.) Simple contradiction, as in this pass. and in III. 1. 22, 52, 60.
(b.) Correction of an inadequate statement, as in IV. 2. 4, IV. 4. 38, or a statement wrong in some particular, as in IV. 3. 40, III. 2. 42.

ACT I.   SCENE IV.   99

(c.) Correction of a negative, in which case it *appears* to have an affirmative force, as III. 1. 138, V. 2. 19. (Ram. Excurs. IV.)

23. **Num non vis** = *num nonvis*, the *non* going with the verb, making it 2d pers. of *nolo*. "You are not unwilling, are you?" So Poen. V. 2. 119, *num nevis?* to which the answer is *sane volo*.

24. **Illi ... optume volo.** See And. Lex. s. v. Comp. Ter. Heaut. V. 2. 6, *tibi bene volo* and *bene volens*. The phrase in the text is simply the superlative.

25. **'Iam.'** A similar interchange of sentiment between two lovers occurs several times in Pl., as in Amph. I. 3. 32, *redibo actutum*. A. *Id 'actutum' diu est.*

28. **Di te ament** is a common form of salutation, as in III. 2. 28, 117, etc.

30. **Probe,** "good!" See I. 1. 4. On *quin*, see I. 3. 16, and on *amabo*, see I. 3. 10.

33. **Hoc,** abl. referring to Call.

33. **Eumpse** = *ipsum*. "Leave him so by himself." Pl. has also *eapse,* nom. and abl., *eopse, eampse*. *Ipse* is for *is-pse*, and these older forms are made by the inflection of the former part of the compound, as in *idem* (*is-dem*). They are therefore more strictly grammatical than the later forms in which the suffix *-pse* is made the vehicle of the case-endings. See M. 82, 4, obs.; A. & G. 101, foot-note; H. 186, 4. Some regard these forms as contractions for *eum-ipsum, eo-ipso,* etc., but with less probability. The form *reapse* is *re-ea-pse*.

34. **Da ab Delphio,** "pass the wine, beginning with Delphium." *Da ab* is the usual order for passing the wine, and the prepos. is followed by the name of the person with whom a beginning is to be made, or as in Asin. V. 2. 41, *da ab summo*.

ACT II. SCENE I.

For the division into Acts, see Intro. At this point the banquet went on without interruption, and it is the opinion of Lorenz that the spectators were entertained with music given by the *tibicen*. Comp. Pseud. I. 5, last line, *tibicen vos interea hic delectaverit*. Tranio, who had gone to the fish market in the Piraeus (I. 1. 63-4, 72), comes back, and pauses at one side of the stage to speak the lines 1-15.

1. **Opibus atque industriis,** "with all his might and main." *Industria* in the plu. is found nowhere except here, and Ram. suggests that it may be a bit of bad grammar used to raise a laugh. That is possible, but abstracts are very commonly used in the plu. by Pl., where class. usage requires the sing., as *superbiae atque irae, gratiae*, etc. (Lor. and Wag.)
2. **Perisse** (*periisse*) = *perditos esse*.
3. **Stabulum ... confidentiae,** "a standing-place for confidence." In the same figurative sense in Aul. II. 2. 56, *stabile stabulum*.
4. **Nobis saluti,** double dat. On the line, which seems proverbial, comp. Capt. III. 3. 14, and Ter. Adelph. IV. 7. 43, *ipsa si cupiat Salus, servare ... non potest*. For the condition *si cupiat ... potest*, see A. & G. 307, *d*; H. 512, 1.
5. **Ad portum,** "at the harbor." So *ad forum,* "at the forum," III. 2. 156, and IV. 4. 7. The construction is not uncommon in Pl. Comp. the regular class. phrase *ad omnia pulvinaria,* "at all the shrines," Cic. Cat. III. 10, 23.
7. **Facere ... lucri,** "to gain." Comp. *compendi facere,* I. 1. 57. *Lucri* is not an appos. of *argenti*, as Ram. says, an explanation which would serve for this passage only. *Aliquantum* is object of *facere*, and *argenti* gen. partit.
8. **Vicem** is used with a gen. or poss. pron., particularly after words which denote an emotion of the mind. It is called adverbial acc. by Madvig, 237, *c*, obs. 3; G. 331, 3; A. & G. 240, *b*; H. 380, 2, and acc. of the part concerned by Roby, 1101, 1102.
9. **Plagipatidae,** from *plaga* + *patior*, with patronymic ending. Coined by Pl. and used also in Capt. III. 1. 12, of parasites.

ACT II. SCENE I. 101

9. **Ferritribaces**, from *ferrum* + τρίβω, "those who wear out iron" in fetters. So *ulmitriba*, Pers. II. 4. 7. These words were doubtless coined by Pl. for comic effect, and for that purpose a hybrid word was used rather than the pure Latin *ferriteri*, which is used in Trin. IV. 3. 14. (See Rost. Opusc. I. 251.)

10. **Trium numorum.** The exact force of these words is a matter of dispute. *Numus* in Pl. means the Attic didrachma whenever it refers to a definite sum, and if that is the case here, *tres numi* means the monthly pay of a Roman soldier. So Ram. takes it. Lor. thinks it is a confusion resulting from carelessness in translating from the Greek In any case, the sum is a small one, ridiculously small in proportion to the danger. The same sum, paid for a trick which involved no risk or labor, gives the name to the Trinummus.

11. **Aliqui**, subj. of *solent*. *Corpus*, acc. of part referred to.

12 sq. Lor. remarks on this passage that Pl. does not shrink from jesting about the most severe punishments. Many phrases, as *abi in malam crucem*, *dierecte*, etc., were used as expletives without much thought of their meaning, and it must be remembered also that these punishments were often threatened, but seldom employed.

13. **Lege**, "on this condition." For explan. of the remainder of this line, see I. 1. 52.

14. **Argentum ... praesentarium**, "ready money," "cash." So IV. 2. 10. The classical word is *praesens*. (Wag.)

15. **Curriculo**, originally an abl., but used by Pl. as an adv., "quickly." Quite common. See And.'Lex. s. v.

16. **Opsonium.** Ὄψον meant anything eaten as a relish with bread, and especially, as here, fish, which was a favorite article of food with the Athenians.

18. **Ted** = *te*. The *d* at the end of this word was frequently used in the early Latin after the abl. of nouns and pron., and seems to have been incorrectly transferred to the acc. *me*, *te*, and perhaps *se*. The extent of its use in Pl. is a matter of doubt, but *med*, *ted* are found a number of times in good MSS.

21. **Quid ego ago? ... Accubas.** Philol. asks the question in bewilderment with about the same sense as *quid agam?* A. & G. 276, *c*; G. 219; M. 339, obs. 2. The pres. for the fut. "when one asks one's self what one must do or think (on the instant)." But Tran. takes it literally and answers, "You are lying at the table?" Thornton's Pl. translates,

> "What am I about?
> *Tra.* A mischief on you! ask what you 're about?
> About your supper —"

Comp. a similar retort in III. 2. 30.

24. **Amolirier** = *amoliri* with pass. sense. So *demolio* is used by Naevius, and many deponent verbs (see I. 3. 10) have an act. form in Pl. (Lor.).

27. **Valeat pater,** "away with his father!" But as *valeo* means originally "to be in good health," Philol. takes it literally and says, "he is indeed in good health." We may render, "Farewell to his father!" PH. "He does indeed fare well, but I am lost."

28. **Bis peristi.** Call., who is only half awake, hears the last word, *disperi*, and mistaking it for *bis peri*, says, "You have perished *twice*? How can that be?" There seems to be no equiv. pun in English.

30. Notice the gradual awakening of Call. from 26, 27, 28, to this line, where he understands the words but fails to grasp the situation, and line 37, where he suffers a relapse into nonsense. Comp. this with the condition of Lepidus, in Ant. and Cleop. Act II. Sc. VII.

32. **Plenas.** There were only three persons, but Philol. uses a natural exaggeration in his excitement.

33. **Igitur demum,** "then." Correlative to *ubi*. So III. 1. 154, *igitur tum ... quando.* Comp. I. 2. 47.

35. **Deposivit.** *Pono* is *po* + *sino*, and *posivi* for *posui* is the earlier form, and the only one used by Pl. and Ter. (Brix.)

36. **Etiam vigilas?** *Etiam* with imperv. or in impatient questions implying an exhortation, may often be best rendered

by the introduction of a negative in Engl. "Will you not wake up?" So IV. 3. 5, *Etiamne aperis?* "Will you not open?" Trin. II. 4. 113, *Etiam tu taces?* "Won't you keep still?" So IV. 1. 27, *etiam aspice*, "look, won't you?" (Ram. Excurs. III. Wag.)

37. **Soleas.** The sandals were removed on reclining at the table, and to call for the sandals (*poscere soleas*, Hor. Sat. II. 8. 77) was an indication of a purpose to leave.

38. **Intro**, "within," i.e., into the house, where Call. would not be seen. Up to this point the feasters have remained in the *vestibulum* or the garden.

39. This line is omitted from the text.

41. **Nullus sum,** "it is all over with me;" more forcible than *perii*, Don. Ter. Andr. 599. See M. 455, obs. 5.

41. **Taceas.** The 2d pers. of pres. subjunc. for imperv. is very rare in class. Latin, except where the subject is indefinite, but is common in comedy to express a friendly command. M. 385, obs.

41. **Qui,** abl. interrog. Join *tibi* with *sedem*.

42. **Satin' habes,** "do you consider it enough?" Comp. the same phrase in a different sense, III. 2. 142.

43. **Non modo ne,** very rare for *ut non modo non*, to introduce a clause of result. M. 456, obs. 4.

44. **Vos,** addressed to the women, as Philol.'s question shows. *Hac* and *istac* in next line also refer to them.

46. **Igitur** here approaches the later sense of logical consequence. "What is it, then?" Tranio's answer leads Delphium to think he is going to send them away.

46. **Non hoc longe.** Accompanied by a gesture, possibly as in several similar places, by pointing to the finger-nail; "not the breadth of my nail." So Ram.

47. **Intus.** This word has three distinct meanings: 1. "Within," ἔνδον, as here and in 54, 55, below. 2. "From within," ἔνδοθεν as in 58 and III. 1. 140. 3. "To a place within" = *intro*, of which there is no example in this play, but common in Lucr. (Ram. Roby.) Comp. *intro*, 43, 44.

47. **Tantillo**, diminutive from the dim. *tantulus*. On formation see M. 182, *b*, and obs. 1; G. 785, 9, *b*.

48. **Quo eveniant** depends upon the idea of thinking implied in *metu*.

48. **Madeo metu.** And. Lex. translates, "to sweat or melt with fear," but it is rather "I am saturated with fear." Comp. Lucr. IV. 792, *arte madent*, "are full of art." So also Hor. and Mart. Possibly the full idea is, "I am saturated to the dripping point."

49. **Potin'** = *potisne*, sc. *est*, "is it possible?" Not 2d pers. for *potesne*. See note on *pote*, I. 3. 99. *Ne* appended to any other word than the verb suggests doubt and indignation, which may often be expressed in Engl. by the use of a negative, as in the corresponding use of *etiam*, line 36. Render, "Can't you be quiet?" So Men. III. 2. 1, *potin' ut quiescas?* "Can't you keep still?" M. 451, *a*.

51. **Morigerae** arises from the construction *morem gerere*, in I. 3. 32.

51. **Ille** is often used with Iuppiter both in comedy and in class. writers, and was perhaps accompanied by a gesture upward.

51. **Faxit.** Old form of fut. subjunc. made in the same way as *faxo*, I. 1. 65, with ending –*im*. The later Latin retained *faxim* and *ausim* (*audeo*). This wish is added as if superhuman aid were needed to make a woman obedient.

53. **Face occlusae sient** = *fac* (*ut*) *sint*, etc. So in next line *cave* (*ne*) *siveris*. In both cases the dependent verb is logically the leading verb, and the independent verb only adds a jussive force. Render, "let the house be shut," and "do not allow." So *fac sciam*, "let me know." Comp. A. & G. 331, *f*, and 269, *a*; G. 264.

55. **Natus nemo**, "not a soul." A Plautine phrase, used again II. 2. 21. Lor. suggests that Cic. would have said *nemo mortalis*. This line and the next depend upon 54; the responses of Philol. do not interrupt the speech.

55. **Licet**, "it shall be done," denoting assent without permission, an idea easily derived from the original sense of *licet*. Comp. Trin. II. 4. 116, *huc concede aliquantum*. Ph. *Licet*. Men.

ACT II. SCENE I. 105

I. 4. 6, *ceterum cura.* C. *Licet.* In each case render, "It shall be done," or "I will."

57. **Numquid aliud,** sc. *vis.* "You don't want anything else, do you?" The ordinary formula for taking leave. So *numquid vis?* Hor. Sat. I. 9. 6.

57. **Clavem Laconicam.** Large three-toothed keys, which locked the door from the outside. No good explanation of the name or of the manner of working has been proposed. It seems probable, from this passage, that a person on the outside could tell whether the door had been locked from within or from without.

58. **Hinc foris,** "from this side, without," so that the house might seem to have been deserted.

59. After this line the others go into the house, leaving Tranio alone.

60–70. These lines are somewhat confused in the MSS. and have been the subject of much conjecture and comment. Particularly, the word *proprior* is read *propior* in several MSS., *probior* in Vulg., and *probrior* by Rit. The best notes on line 60 are by Taubmann, Lorenz, Rost (Opusc. I. 135) and Ritschl, but they are widely at variance with each other.

The general sense of this passage is this: It makes no difference who a man is, if he lack courage. Any man can act foolishly on short notice, but it requires a wise man to bring good results out of things which have been foolishly begun.

60. **Pluma** seems to be a nom. So twice in Ter. with *interest.*

60. **Cluens** = *cliens.* Render, "whether patron or client be the rôle assigned to a man," etc.

61. **Quoi,** the orig. form from stem *quo–* of *qui.* *Qu–* was often used for *c* (comp. *cocus,* I. 3. 120), and about 200 B. C. there was a general weakening of *o* to *u.* The form *coi* does not appear, and the two changes seem to have taken place together in this word. So *quoius, cujus.*

62. **Homini,** dat. after *facile est.* *Optumo* and *pessumo* repeat the idea of *patronus* and *cluens.*

63. **Quamvis desubito,** "on however short a notice" (Ram.).

63. **Nequiter** is without moral force. Simply "foolishly," i. e., so as to produce bad results. So *nequitia*, 65, "folly."
64. **Id**, that is, *ni patiatur* and *ut proveniant*. *Opus* in the orig. sense, "the work of a wise man."
65. **Quae.** The anteced. is *cuncta*. Render, "all those things which have been planned and acted upon foolishly."
67. This line precedes 66 in the MSS. and Ram. The order of the text is that given by Acidal. Rit. Weise. Lor. Bothe.
67. **Ni** = *ne*. The oldest inscriptions and best MSS. vary between *nei*, *ni*, and *ne*, the first being rather more frequent in the time of Pl. Comp. *-eis*, *-es*, and *is* in acc. plu. 3d decl. Render the line, "that he (the *vir doctus*) may not suffer anything on account of which he shall be sorry to live," i. e., "shall wish he were dead."
69. **Liqueant**, "be clear." The figure in these two lines is that of wine which has been disturbed and needs to settle again. So V. 1. 11, *turbida*, and often in Pl.
71. **Tu**, addressed to the boy. Tran. does not remember that he had asked for the key, and is alarmed at the appearance of the slave. But when he sees the key, he recalls his purpose, and speaks approvingly. *O* is his exclamation upon seeing the key.
72. **Maxumo opere**, "most emphatically," the superl. of *magnopere*.
73. **Orare**, sc. *me*. The common omission of the subject. So with *facturum*, 75, sc. *me*, and with *venire*, 78, sc. *eum*.
76. **Capite obvoluto.** The Greeks and Romans veiled the head by covering it with a corner of the robe, when they were in desperate circumstances or in great crises. So Cæsar, when he could no longer defend himself, and Socrates when he felt death coming upon him.
78. **Hinc**, as before, "from this side." After these words, the boy goes in and Tran. locks the door.
79-80. **Ludos ... seni faciam.** The phrase *ludos facere alicui*, "to perform games in honor of any one," must be distinguished from the phrase *ludos facere aliquem*, "to make

ACT II. SCENE II. 107

sport of any one." Both are taken from the public or funeral games, and *ludos* is therefore always plural. (Comp. *ludus fit* in Argument.) The former expression is used ironically by Pl., as here, and then does not differ much in meaning from the latter.

80. **Quod** refers to the preceding clause, "a thing which." On the attempt to fix the date of the play by these words, see Introduction.
81. **Huc, hinc.** Tran. goes away from the door of the house, that he may not seem to have come from it.
82. **Sarcinam**, i. e., a load of deceit, which Theuropides will carry if he believes the story of Tran. The same figure is used in III. 2. 89.

ACT II. SCENE II.

Theuropides comes upon the stage, followed by slaves (*pedisequi*) who carry the rugs and other baggage, used on the journey from which Theuropides has just returned. Tranio is not seen at first by the others, and stands at one side watching them.

2. **Quom**, "inasmuch as," with indic., is especially frequent in thanksgivings.
2. **Amisisti** = *dimisisti*, as often in Pl. So Mil. Glor. IV. 3. 3, Men. V. 8. 6.
2. **Modo** emphasizes *vix*, "scarcely even alive." So in next line, "only."
3. **Pedem latum**, by hendiadys for *pedis latitudinem*. Taken by Lor. as acc. of extent of space, with *me* supplied as obj. of *inposisse;* it may, however, be direct obj.
4. **Inposisse**, for *inposivisse* = later *imposuisse*. See note on *deposivit*, II. 1. 35.
6. **Apage**, "get out!" "away with you!" "I want no more to do with you." In the same sense in a similar expression of thankfulness in Trin. IV. 1. 19.
7. **Crediturus ... fui.** "I intended to trust." M. 342, *a*; G. 239.
8. **Largiter.** The classical form is *large*. The ending *-iter* is

more commonly used with adjs. of 3d decl. (M. 198, *b* and obs. 2.), but Pl. frequently uses it with adjs. of 2d decl. (Wag. Trin. 1060.)

10. **Aegupto.** For spelling comp. *gumnastica*, I. 2. 66. The construction would generally, but not invariably, require a prepos. in good prose. Pl. is especially free in his construction with names of places.
11. **Expectatus,** "eagerly looked for." *Optatus,* Lamb.
14. The house-doors were shut but not locked during the day, and the *ianitor* was always ready to open them when any one came. (Lamb.) Similar expressions of surprise at finding the house shut in the daytime occur in Stich. II. 1. 36, sqq.
14. **Interdius,** "in the daytime." This word is found five times in Pl., and is from *dius,* an old form of *dies.* Comp. *diurnus, nudiustertius, sub diu,* and the adv. *diu.*
15. This line is accompanied by violent knocking. Comp. 25. The next line is spoken as Tran. comes forward, and is intended to be overheard.
19. **Vsque invaluisti?** "Have you been well up to this time?"
20. **Quidum,** "how then?" This word usually stands by itself, as here, and asks for an explanation of what has preceded.
23. **Pultando.** *Pultare* is the regular word for knocking at the door. This was often, perhaps always, done with the feet, and sometimes with great violence. Comp. IV. 1. 39–40.
23. **Ambas.** The *fores* were double folding-doors.
24. **An.** See note on I. 1. 7.
25. **Quin.** See I. 3. 16, *c.* An impatient correction of the expectation implied in the preceding question. "(Touched it!) Why, more than that, I have almost broken," etc.
28. **Facinus,** in the original sense of "deed," which is the usual one in Pl.
29. **Quid,** acc. of specif. "How now?"
30. Notice the effect of the repetition of *tetigistin'* in increasing the fright of Theur., and the fact that Tran. gives no explanation until he has called the slaves away. Notice also that the story is finally told in the most confused way, as if Tran.

were still afraid that some evil would come to them. This scene would gain greatly by being put upon the stage.

32. **Occidisti hercle.** After these words Tran. pauses as if in fear, intentionally breaking off his speech at a critical point.

33. **Cum isto omine,** "with that prophecy of bad luck," implied in the foregoing words. Comp. Ter. Hec. I. 2. 59, *At te di deaeque faxint cum isto odio* (Lor.), and observe the use of the subj. in *-sim* in wishes, as II. 1. 51.

34. **Expiare,** "to free from guilt." Notice the neg. effect of *ut* after verbs of fearing. "I wish that you may, but fear that you may not." *Istos* refers to the slaves.

37. **Ne attigatis.** A prohibition in 2d pers. would regularly stand in the perf. subjunc. (A. & G. 269, *a*, *b*; G. 266, 267) or fut. perf. (M. 386, and obs. 1, last clause). But Pl. and Ter. very frequently use the present, as I. 3. 58, *ne suadeas*, and the common phrase *molestus ne sis*. *Attigatis* is from the early form *tago* for *tango*. Comp. As. II. 2. 106, *si me tagis*.

38. **Tangite vos quoque terram.** *Quoque* goes with *vos*, "you also" (as I do). To touch the earth with the hand was a religious observance in speaking of the dead or any kindred subject, and was a protection against evil results.

40. **Tetulit.** Reduplicated for *tulit*. The usual form in Pl., as Amph. II. 2. 84, 168, etc.

41. **Numquis est.** A good example of a question which may be either direct or indirect, and which illustrates the transition from one construction to the other.

42. **Aucupet.** Act. for depon. form, as often in Pl.

43. **Etiam,** "again." "Having done it once, do it even now a second time." Comp. the analogous use of *etiam* in I. 2. 34.

44. **Capitalis caedis** (-*es*), "a horrible murder." *Capitalis* refers to the death of the victim, not to the punishment inflicted upon the murderer. (Ram.)

44. **Intellego.** The spelling *intelligo* is without good MSS. authority, and is rejected from the text of Cic. by Halm and Wilkins. See Fleck. *Ep. ad Rit.* viii.

45. **Antiquom et vetus.** The distinction between these words must be observed here. See And. Lex. *antiquus*.
46. **Adeo,** "and so," "therefore." "It was done long ago, and so we have just found it out." *Vetus* in this line would give the wrong sense.
50. **Hospiti,** dat. of disadvantage for abl. of separation. H. 385, 4; A. & G. 229; G. 344, 2.
53–55. **Cenaverat ... redit ... abimus ... condormivimus.** Tran. begins his story with the plupf., the natural tense, but the excitement hurries him into the pres. and perf. definite. Such change of tense is characteristic of dialogue. (Lor.)
53. **Cenaverat ... cena.** This spelling is preferable to that with *coen–*, which is founded upon a mistaken etymol. *Foris cenaverat,* "had dined out;" *foras cenare,* "to go out to dinner." Comp. I. 1. 1.
57. **Atque,** "and then." *Ille* refers to Philol., as appears from 58, but is left indefinite by Tran. to increase the fear and confusion of Theur.
58. **An gnatus meus?** "Not my son, was it?" See note on I. 1. 7, and comp. I. 4. 20.
58. **St.** The same particle is used as a sign of silence in Epid. II. 2. 1, *st, st, tace,* and in line 74 of this scene.
59. **Illum ... mortuom,** "the dead man of whom I have spoken." Comp. the use of the Greek article, and see H. 450, 4; A. & G. 102, *b*; G. 292, 1.
60. **Nempe** was used to confirm what had been said, but often, as here, ironically, to express the contrary sense and cast doubt upon a previous statement.
60. **In somnis,** "in his sleep." Comp. Virg. Aen. III. 151, where some have written as one word *insomnis*. But see Forbiger's note.
62. **Mirum, quin.** This common Plautine phrase expresses great contempt for some previous statement. The literal sense is "it is wonderful how not," but it may be rendered often ironically, "it is very likely that." Amph. II. 2. 118, *mirum quin te advorsus dicat,* "it is wonderful that he (your slave)

does not contradict you," "it is likely, I suppose, that your slave would contradict you." So Cist. IV. 2. 67, where a box is lost and the owner says it is of no great value, the answer is, *mirum quin grex venalium in cistella infuerit una,* "it is wonderful, I suppose, that there should not be a troop of slaves in one little box." So Merc. I. 1. 19, Pers. III. 1. 1, etc. This is to be distinguished from *mirum ni*, which expresses genuine surprise.

The sense of this passage therefore is, "In his dreams? Of course it was in his dreams. You would not expect a man who had been dead sixty years to appear to another who was wide awake!"

63. **Abhinc sexaginta annis.** "*Abhinc* is used with the abl. in two passages only (Pl. Most. 494; [this passage] C. Verr. 2. 52) and in these it means 'from *that* time.'" (Roby.) In other cases *abhinc* takes acc. of duration of time. The ordinary expression here would be *ante sex. annis* or *annos*. H. 427, and 1, M. 270, and obs. 4.

64. This line as it stands is incorrect in metre. Rit. following one MS. writes in two lines:—

Interdum inepte stultus es [Theuropides].
TH. Taceo. TR. Set ecce quae illi ille inquit [mortuos].

65. **Diapontius** is of course a fanciful name, the Greek equiv. of *transmarinus*.

67. **Acheruntem** is the earlier form for *Acherons, -ontis.* So *Acherusius* for *Acherontius*. The word has generally the construction of the name of a town, though below, line 76, it is used with *ad*. (Lor.) *Orcus* is here the name of the god.

68. **Praemature**, i. e., by a violent death, which cut short the natural term of life.

70. **Defodit insepultum.** These words do not contradict each other. *Defodit* refers to the burial of the body; *insepultum*, to the omission of due funeral rites, without which the burial was not complete. Comp. the episode of Polydorus, Virg. Aen. III, 20–68.

72. **Scelestae**, "polluted." So Virg. Aen. III, 60-61, *scelerata . . . terra . . . pollutum hospitium*.

74. **St, st!** At this point some one within the house comes to the door, and Tran. utters this sound both to warn the person within and to frighten Theur. still further.

74. **Concrepuit.** This is the regular word used to indicate that some one is coming out from the house. Very common in Pl. and Ter. It has been explained by supposing that, as the street doors opened outward upon the sidewalk, any one coming out rattled the door in order to warn passers. Another explanation, supported by a number of passages in Curc., as I. 1. 20, refers the word to the creaking of the door. The singular is used because only one of the *valvae* was ordinarily opened.

75. **Hicine**, i. e., the ghost. For form see I. 1. 8. Tran. turns the danger to good account by making Theur. believe that it is the ghost within who is coming to the door to see who knocked. With the rest of the line comp. the phrase *exsanguis metu*, Ov. Met. IX, 224.

76. **Accersunt.** This is the best MS. reading for *arcessunt*. See And. Lex.

77. **Illisce**, those within the house. This form of the nom. rests upon the concurrent testimony of inscriptions, manuscripts and grammarians. *Hisce* (nom.) is found in Ter. Eun. II. 2. 38, in Trin. IV. 2. 36, Pseud. I. 5. 125, and several other places, and in Mil. Glor. II. 4. 21, *hisce oculis* (nom.). The inscriptions give also the endings *–eis, es* of 2d decl. nouns. *Illisce* may be the correct form in IV. 3. 3. (Brix. Roby.)

78. **Nimis quam,** "very greatly." *Quam* is used with *nimis* as with superlatives. Capt. I. 2. 17, *nimis quam cupio*. So with *valde, sane, mire*.

79. Theur. does not understand the words of the two preceding lines, but his suspicion is aroused, and he asks for an explanation. Tran. only redoubles his efforts to get him from the door.

82. **Heus, Tranio!** These words are by Rost and Lorenz sup-

posed to be spoken by some one within, but most editors give them to Theur. because of what follows in 85, sq. In either case Tran. pretends to think that they are spoken by the ghost, and so adapts his next words, which are spoken in a loud voice, as to give warning to those within and at the same time to increase the fear of Theur. by appearing to believe that the ghost is calling to him. Line 83 is an exculpation of himself addressed to the ghost.

85. **Tu** is expressed for emphasis. Render, "It was *you* who called me, was it?" For this use of *an* see I. 1. 7, and for tense see I. 3. 54.
86. **Amabunt.** The fut. indic. in a wish is not uncommon in Pl. and Ter. Comp. Ter. Heaut. III. 1. 54, *sic me di amabunt*. This is analogous to the fut. indic. for the imperative. (See below, 94.) The other form of the wish, *ita me di ament*, has occurred in I. 3. 14.
88. **Etiamne astas?** "Do you still stand near?"
89. **Respexis**, formed like *faxit*, II. 1. 51, for *respec-sis*. The fut. subj. in *-sim* is especially frequent in wishes or in prohibitions with *cave* (*ne*). So Aul. IV. 2. 1. *cave cuiquam indicassis*, and *curassis*, 92.
91. **Quid modo igitur?** "Only what then? why," etc. Tranio's evident fear at line 78 recurs to the mind of Theur., and brings back his suspicion.
93. **Vt occepisti**, in line 80 and perhaps 30 of this scene. *Quis* from *queo*.
94. **Herculem.** Hercules is to be invoked as the god who wards off evil, and particularly as the one who had descended to the lower world and returned in safety. (Lor.)
94. **Invocabis.** The use of the fut. indic. for imperative indicates "a firm conviction that the command or direction will be complied with." M. 384, obs.; H. 470, 1; G. 265, 1; A. & G. 269, *f*. It is used for greater vividness. See note on I. 1. 9.
94. **Hercules.** The full name is used in this invocation, as the forms *hercle*, *mehercle*, had become mere expletives, which

8

did not express an appeal to the god. With these words Theur. covers his head and runs off the stage, followed by his slaves.

95. **Et ego**, sc. *Herculem invoco*.

97. **Malum** is to be taken with *quid*. "What a mischief of a business," etc. This is a somewhat unusual sense for *quid malum*, and *malus* and *mali* have been conjectured.

ACT III. SCENE I.

While Tranio is speaking the last lines of the scene, the danista comes upon the stage looking for Philolaches.

1. **Scelestiorem**, "more villanous." (Ram.)

1. **Faenori** is the spelling of the best MSS., though *fenus* is also found. The dat. *faenori* is used after verbs of borrowing and lending, and comes under the general head of dat. of end or purpose. Roby suggests that it may be a locative. Comp. V. 3. 19, *faenori argentum sumere*, and the phrase *dono dare*. The abl. is more common, as in III. 1. 69, IV. 2. 14.

1. **Argento**, sc. *locando* (Lamb.), "for investing money at interest."

3. **Mani**. The MSS. give *mane* here and in III. 2. 78, but *mani* is generally adopted on the authority of Servius, Aen. I. 19. It is an archaic locative, like *vesperi, luci, temperi*.

4. **Nemini** = *apud neminem*. (Lor.)

5-15. Tran. speaks these lines in a low tone so that he is not heard by the banker, and is hoping to escape unnoticed, until he sees Theur. coming from the other side (line 10).

5. **In perpetuom modum**. See note on I. 2. 62. "I am undone without anything to check my downward course."

7. **Amica**, *Philematium*. *Quo* abl. after *opus*. Part of the money was used for current expenses.

8. **Nisi quod**, "unless;" but rare in this sense, for which reason some editors read *nisi quid*. "Unless I first prevent the old man from hearing of this now."

ACT III. SCENE I. 115

9. **Huic** refers to the danista, but in next line *hic* refers to Theur. Such use of the same pronoun to refer to different persons would hardly be found in careful prose, but is natural in conversation, where the speaker turns from one person to another, so that each in turn becomes *hic* to him. So *iste*, 134, 135 of this scene.

11. **Indaudiverit** = *inaud-*. The old form *indu* (*indo*) for *in* is used by Pl. only in this verb. Comp. Aul. II. 2. 88, Capt. Prol. 30, etc. It is found in Lucr. and in the XII. Tables, and remained in classical Latin in the words *indigeo* (*indu-egeo*), *indigena*, *indipiscor*. (Lor.) Also *indoles*, *industria*.

13. **Animus hominis conscius.** *Hominis* is poss. gen. with *animus*. With *conscius* supply *sibi mali*. The absolute use of *conscius* with *mali* understood is found in later Latin, and survives in the Engl. "conscience," i. e., "consciousness of evil."

15. **Turbare**, "to create confusion," as in V. I. 12, where the same idea is more fully expressed, viz., that one who is already in difficulty should seek to increase the confusion in order to escape unnoticed.

16. **Vnde is?** "Whence do you come?" though *ire* in this sense is rare. Comp. Cas. II. 3. 29. The words are addressed to Theur.

16. **Vnde** = *a quo* (masc.). So also IV. 4. 5, and *hinc* = *ab hoc*, III. 1. 113. Similar usages are found in good prose. (Lor.) M. 317, obs. 2.

17. **Illo**, the story about the murder. Notice that *numquid*, implying a negative, is met by *hercle vero* and by the emphatic position of *dixi*.

19. **Techinae** = *technae*, for τέχναι. This is the reading of the best MSS., though Ram. has *technae*. Some Greek combinations were avoided in the Latin, particularly in the early writers, by the insertion of a short vowel. Thus χμ, κμ, were separated by ŭ, as δραχμή, *drachuma*; χν, κν, μν, by ĭ, as μνᾶ, *mina*; and κλ by ŏ. (Lor. Rit.)

20. **Enim** frequently implies an ellipsis of the leading clause.

Comp. *nam*, I. 3. 34. Here the sense is "(Why do you ask) for I said nothing." *Nihil enim* is used with the same ellipsis in Ter. Hec. V. 4. 10, Adelph. IV. 5. 22, and this is especially frequent in negations. See M. 454, obs. 2. Comp. IV. 2. 23, V. 3. 12, 23. (See Ram. Excurs. VI.)

21. **Dixtine** = *dixistine*. Pl. uses either form.
22. **Imo.** Comp. note on I. 4. 22, (*a*). "No, on the contrary, he strongly denies it." It has been suggested (Collins, Pl. for Engl. Readers) that Pl. here gives a hint of an amusing scene, in which Theur. charges the former owner of the house with the murder of his guest, and is met by indignant denials.
24. **Dicam, si confessus sit.** *Dicam* is pres. subj. The context shows that non-fulfilment is intended, and the usual form would be *dicerem, si confessus esset*. Comp. Pers. II. 2. 33, *fatear, si ita sim*, Epid. III. 1. 10, *si . . . habeam, pollicear*. In both passages it appears from the context that the supposition is contrary to fact. The pres. is used for the imperf. or plup. subj. to indicate non-fulfilment, "by a turn of rhetoric, where a thing is represented as if it might still take place." M. 347, *b*, obs. 1. Read also A. & G. 308, foot-note.
25. **Egon'.** The leading clause is omitted, and *ne* is appended to the first word of the subordinate clause. The full form would be *Rogasne, quid ego censeam?* Comp. III. 2. 50.
26. **Iudicem**, an arbitrator, who would save the expense and trouble of a lawsuit.
27. This line is spoken as an "aside."
29. **Tranium.** Elsewhere in the Most. the regular form in *-o, -onis*, is used, of which *Tranium* is probably a diminutive. So *Philematium* is a dim. from *Philematio*, which is found in nom., gen., and dat. in inscriptions. (Lor.) *Neque faenus neque sortem*, "neither interest nor principal."
31. **Quo te agis?** On seeing the banker coming toward him, Tran. starts to go away, and causes the question of Theur. He is detained by this, and has no resource but to go toward the danista. Lines 32-36 are spoken aside. The banker

ACT III. SCENE I. 117

stands watching the house of Philol., which Theur. does not dare to approach.

31. **Nec** has no connective force. Comp. I. 3. 83.
33. **Illo** refers to Theur. The subject of *adibit* is *danista*.
33. **Ne** (= *nae*) is the spelling of the best MSS.
34. **Exhibent negotium,** "cause trouble."
36. **Frustra,** "in error," the original sense. See And. Lex. for etymol., and comp. Amph. III. 3. 19, *hi ambo frustra sunt*, where *errant probe* is added as synonymous. So very often in Pl.
37. **Iubeo** is used with reference to the imperative in the common salutation *salve*. Comp. Engl. "I bid you farewell."
37. **Misargurides.** For etymol. see Intro. The MSS. give various forms, and this is taken from Donat. in Ter. Adel.
39. **Pilum.** Notice the Roman metaphor, which must have been added by Pl.
40. **Inanis.** Tranio's manner shows that he is not intending to pay the debt. These words are spoken aside, but overheard by Tran.
40. **Hariolus** is generally used by Pl. to mean a *true* prophet. So Asin. III. 2. 33, *ariolare*, "you speak the truth." (Ram.)
41. **Quin** is repeated by Tran. as a sort of repartee. Such a use is quite frequent, as in Cas. III. 4. 9, sqq., where two old men in a wrangle repeat *quin* at the beginning of a dozen successive retorts. *Mittis*, "put aside," "have done with."
45. Tranio is endeavoring to invent some story which will get the banker out of the way, and keep him quiet while he remains.
46. **Hercle vero.** Comp. line 18, with note.
49. **Reddetur.** This promise has of course no foundation, and is given only as a temporary expedient. It is generally characteristic of the slaves in Pl. to adopt such expedients on the spur of the moment, and thereby involve themselves in greater difficulties. Comp. the story told in 104, sq.
52. **Imo,** "no, on the contrary," etc.
53. **Vos,** Tran. and Philol. as in 30.
54. Beginning with this line, Ritschl rearranges the lines of this

scene down to 77 in the following order: 54, 57, 55, a conjectural line, 56, 61–68, 58, 59, 60, 70, 72, 73, 69, 74, 75, 76, 71, 77. See Parerg. I. 493–500. Lorenz has a different arrangement.

54. **Eu hercle.** The line has been emended in various ways, but we may consider these words ironical, as is *euge strenue*, and retain them in the text.

55. **Nominabo.** A reference to the *pipulum*, which was a privilege granted to a creditor by the XII Tables. In default of written evidence of the debt, he could go to the house of the debtor and demand payment with loud and abusive language. Comp. Pseud. IV. 7. 46, *flagitare saepe clamore in foro, quom libella nusquam est. Libella* is the written evidence. (Ram. Hild. Lor.)

57. **Frustramini** from the orig. meaning of *frustra*, as above, 36. Notice that *iam multos dies* gives the force of the perf. tense to the verb, as *iampridem* would do. "You have been cheating."

59. **Hoc verbo eripis.** This is the reading of the best MSS. and is retained in the text, though its meaning is not quite certain. No satisfactory conjecture has been offered. It may be, "By this word (i. e., by doing what this phrase means, by paying me the money) you take away from me all ground for dunning you." This seems to be the understanding of Lor. Rost reads *verbum eripit*, in which case the sense would be, "This proposition takes away from you the possibility of giving an evasive answer." The verse is discussed in Rit. Parerg. I, 502, Rost. Opusc. I, 136.

60. **Sortem accipe,** "take the principal." Tran. makes the offer in order to quiet the creditor by an appearance of ability to pay part of the debt.

60. **Imo faenus,** "no, give me the interest." The acceptance of the principal alone might have weakened the claim to the interest.

62. **Extentatum,** supine from *extento*, intens. of *extendo*. "To stretch your lungs with shouting." This verb is found in only

ACT III. SCENE I.   119

two other passages before the post-class. writers, viz., Bacch. IV. 2. 3, and Lucr. III. 489. (Ram.)

62. **In manu,** "in your power." So Merc. III. 4. 43, *tibi in manu est.*

63. **Ne γρῦ quidem,** "not even a grunt can you get from him," i. e., from Philol. Οὐδὲ γρῦ is used in this way by Aristoph. and Dem. (Lor.)

64–66. These lines are much mutilated in the MSS., and the conjectures, by which Cam. filled the blanks, do not make a very perfect text.

65. **Hic,** Philol. Before *linquat,* sc. *ut.* "That he shall leave the city, being made an exile for your sake? he, who will scarcely be able to pay the principal?"

66. **Quin.** "Why, I tell you, I do not ask for the principal."

74. **Veterator.** A conj. of Cam. The word is not found in Pl., but is used by Ter. and Cic. The orig. meaning is an old slave, opposed to *novitius,* and hence one who is old in rascality. "Old sharper."

75. **Quemquam** agrees as an adj. pron. with *beluam.* The masc. *quisquam* is several times used by Pl. with fem. nouns. So Rud. I. 3. 75, *anum quemquam,* Mil. Glor. IV. 2. 68, *quemquam porculam.* So also *quisque, quisquis* and *quis* are used in masc. forms with fem. nouns. (Lor.)

76. **Edepol** is made up of prefix *e–* (*ecastor, equirine*), the voc. of *deus, dee, de,* and the shortened form of *Pollux.* (Lor.) The Roman grammarians spelled it *aedepol,* and derived it from *aedis Pollucis.*

77. Theur. has been standing at a distance, but overhearing some part of the dispute, particularly the word *faenus,* which the Danista had shouted out loudly in 70, 72, he comes up to investigate. The next four lines are spoken rapidly in an undertone, as Theur. crosses the stage.

80. **Inconciliare.** Key, followed by Wag. and Roby, suggests a derivation from *cilium,* "a small hair." The verb would then mean "to entangle," "to involve in difficulties." Ram. gives it, "to raise a disturbance against." Either meaning

will suit the three places where Pl. uses it, better than the definition in And. Lex.

80. **Postules**, "seek," "desire," as in I. 3. 102.

81. **Quin feram.** "Well, you may be sure, I will take it." See I. 3. 16, (*c*).

82. **Quid ais tu? Quid vis?** These two questions are very frequently used together by Pl. The first is meant to attract attention, the second to show on the part of the person addressed that he is listening, and then follows the main question, to which it was desired to call attention. Comp. Trin. I. 2. 159, IV. 2. 85–86. *Quid ais tu?* therefore means, "What do you say to the question I am going to ask?" (Wag.)

86. **Obici ... ob os.** An unusual construction for the dat. The form *obicio* for *objicio* is not given by And. Lex., but is adopted in a number of texts to the exclusion of *objicio*. The answer is intended to suggest that the sum is so small that Theur. can pay it without troubling himself to inquire into the matter at all.

88. In the following lines down to 100, the order of Ritschl has been followed. 89–92 stand in the MSS. after 95, and 98–99, with a repetition of 97, after 117.

91. **Qui sit, unde sit.** Indirect questions in appos. with *istuc*. *Qui* for *quis*, as often. *Vnde sit* refers to *genus*, 90, and may be rendered "of what class he is."

93. **Est.** This word is omitted by most editors, as merely a repetition of the preceding word. But we may suppose that Tran. begins his answer in a way which would lead to too full a statement, and therefore breaks it off.

94. **Quasi**, "about."

95. **Paulum.** The *mina* was equal to about $18, which would make the whole sum $720. Thirty minae were used to buy the freedom of Philem., and the rest were for general expenses. Comp. III. 1. 7, and V. 3. 38–39.

96. **Adeo etiam**, "besides this I hear that interest also is due." *Quatuor*, in next line, the interest.

ACT III. SCENE I. 121

103. **Eo ... argento,** "What has been done with that money?" Comp. *me,* I. 3 65.

103. **Salvom est.** Tran. has, of course, no answer ready, and is gaining time to arrange a new story, but Theur. takes the answer to mean that the money has not been spent.

106. **Patrissat,** "takes after his father." Gr. πατριάζειν. Comp. *badisso,* βαδίζω.

106. **In mercatura vortitur,** "is engaged in trade," a middle sense. *Vorsatur* would more commonly be used, but comp. V. 1. 10, *vorti rem in meo foro.*

107. **Quoiusmodi.** The meaning is "how fine," and this was probably expressed by tone and gesture. (Lor.)

109. **Speculo claras,** "bright as a mirror, pure brightness!" *Speculo* may be taken as an abl. after some such word as *adaeque* or *magis,* understood. *Claras* modifies *aedes* supplied from 107. On account of the irregular construction of *speculo* Rit. supposes that a line has dropped out.

110. **Destinat.** This verb usually means in Pl. either "to fix upon for buying," or "to fix a price upon" and so "to buy." Comp. Rud. Prol. 45. (Ram.)

111. **Talentis magnis.** The Attic talent, which was sixty pounds weight of silver, and was never coined, was worth about $1080. The talent was equal to sixty minae. The adj. *magnum* or the gen. *argenti* was added to distinguish the Attic talent of silver from the Sicilian talent of copper, which was the first known to the Romans, and was of small value. The use of these terms is made clear in Rud. V. 2. 43, 45, 49, and V. 3. 19, 24.

112. **Arraboni,** spelled *arrhabo* by later writers, but see note on *pulcere,* I. 1. 51. Gr. ἀρραβών. The distinction between *arrabo* and *pignus* (And. Lex. s. v.) is not observed in this play. Comp. IV. 3. 39.

113. **Hinc,** from the banker. *Ei* refers to the owner of the house, not yet mentioned by name.

116. **Meridies,** the time when Tran. had promised that the debt should be paid. Comp. 48.

117. **Enecet** may be compared to *intellego* in retaining *e* of the stem. In *enicasso*, I. 3. 55, 66, the added syllables seem to cause the shortening of the vowel. *Vomitum*, "this disgusting fellow."

118. **Adulescens.** The form *adolescens* has much less MS. authority, and is generally rejected from texts of class. writers. The word is used by Pl without reference to age to indicate familiarity, or by a superior to an inferior in station, as here. So Engl. "my lad." (Ram.) See example in next note.

118. **Mecum rem habe,** "treat with me in the matter," i. e., "look to me for your money." Comp. Men. III. 2. 29, *adulescens, quaeso, quid tibi mecum est rei?* "My lad, what's your business with me?" where *adulescens* is addressed to an inferior in station.

118. **Aps** = *abs*. The *s* at the end of this word was appended for euphony before *t*, *c* (*qu*) and sometimes *p*, and for the same reason *b* was in the early writers changed to *p*. The form *abs* was retained by later writers only in the phrase *abs te*.

119. The promise of Theur., a merchant in good standing, is sufficient to satisfy the creditor, who now goes off the stage.

120. **Duint** = *dant*. The Plautine forms *duam, duim, creduam, interduo*, etc., and *duitor* in XII Tables, point to an old form *duo* for *do*. M. 115, *f*; A. & G. 128, *e*, 2; H. 239, 3; G. 191, 3.

121. **Penissume** (*paen-*) is formed by Pl. from *paene*. So from *penitus* the adj. *penitissumus*. (Lor.)

123. **Danisticum** is found only in this passage.

125. **Dicisne.** The impatient tone in which this is spoken gives to *ne* almost the force of *nonne*. Comp. *manesne*, IV. 1. 29, and the force of *etiam*, II. 1. 36. See M. 451, *a*; H. 346, II, 1. 1). Comp. Engl. "Are you going to tell me?"

126. **Quaero,** "I am trying to think."

127. **Comminiscere** retains invariably in Pl. the original sense, "to think up," "to recall," though, as might be expected, the context often shows that some trickery is the object of the thinking. In several passages *comminiscor* cannot mean "to

ACT III. SCENE I.   123

128. **Nisi ut,** sc. *id agam.* See And. Lex. for examples of this ellipsis. After *ut* Lamb. supplies *conferam*, which Rit. adopts in the text. *Hunc vicinum* is Simo, and Tran. means that he will turn the lie over upon Simo by saying that it is his house which Philol. has bought.

"feign," e. g., Aul. I. 1. 30, 37, Bacch. IV. 9. 58. Render, "Come, think it up then."

131. **Calidum** is used in its original sense here, while in 130 it is in the derived sense of "ready," "quick." This line, 131, stands in the MSS. after 76, where it makes no sense at all; it was transferred to this place by Acid. followed by most later editors. There seems to be no equivalent play upon words in English.

131. **Etsi . . . male.** The meaning is : Although its results are far in the future, it hurts me already, I already begin to feel the effects of it.

132. **Quid dei dicunt,** as if whatever comes suddenly into the mind (*calidum*) is an inspiration from the gods.

133. **Istum,** Simo. So in Trin. IV. 2. 78, the Sycophanta curses Charmides because he cannot remember his name. In next line *istunc* refers to Theur. and the words are spoken aside. Comp. the use of *hic* in III. 1. 9, 10.

135. **Bonan' fide,** sc. *emit.* "Has he made a binding contract?" Theur. is afraid that Philol., in his inexperience, may have omitted some necessary part of the bargain.

136. **Redditurus** is used of paying a debt because that was paying back money received, and so transferred to the payment of money for any purpose.

138. **Imo.** See note on I. 4. 22, (*c*). *Imo* contradicts *non perbono.* "On the contrary, he has bought in a very good locality."

142. **Unum.** Traces occur in Pl. of a use of *unus* for the indefinite article, a use which probably continued in vulgar Latin, and gave rise to Italian *uno,* French *un.* Comp. German *ein,* English *an.* So in this play IV. 3. 44, and IV. 4. 9. Render "against a rock," the figure being that of a ship. (Ram.)

144. **Ocius** for positive *ociter*, which is rare. So Ter. Hor. Caes.

145. **Circumducat,** sc. *ut. Ducere, ductare, perductare,* and *perductari,* are also used in the same sense in this play. (Ram.)
145. **Heus tu.** Tran. begins to call, but suddenly thinks of an excuse for stopping. The rest of the line refers to Attic customs, which would not allow a stranger to come into communication with the women of the household.
146. **Utrum** ... –ne, an. M. 452, obs. 1; H. 346, II, 1, 1); G. 460.
147. **Oras** in orig. sense, "to say," "to speak." The same phrase is used in Rud. I. 2. 94. So Virg. Aen. X, 96, *Talibus orabat Juno.* Wag. compares the ordinary meaning of *orator.*
148. **Dum exis,** "until you come out." We might expect the subjunc., but see M. 369, obs. 3; and 339, obs. 2, *b.* The indic. is very common in Pl. with *dum* after verbs of waiting. G. 573.
152. **Concessero.** The fut. perf. is particularly common where some one does something, while something else is taking place. (Lor.)
149-154. Tranio, while speaking these lines, goes away, as if to make inquiries, but in reality to invent an excuse for asking Simo to admit Theur. to the house.

ACT III. SCENE II.

Simo stands in front of his house while the *cantor* chants lines 1-21, which constitute the second *canticum.* Tranio is not seen by Simo, but remains in sight of the spectators. Theuropides goes off the stage at line 148 of the last scene, and does not appear again till line 95.

1. **Melius ... mihi non fuit,** "I have not been better treated" or "better off." Comp. I. 1. 49, *mihi bene est,* and Truc. IV. 2. 28, *bene sumus.*
2. **Nec quod,** sc. *fuit.* "Nor has it happened that," etc. *Una,* "any one meal," "a single meal."
5. **Non ... forte** in this emphatic use is peculiar to Pl. "Not by chance," i. e., for some purpose. Comp. οὐκ ἀλόγως, and the phrase *non temere,* e. g., Aul. IV. 3. 1, *non temere est, quod,* "it is not a matter of chance that," etc. So *non nihilo,* "not for nothing." (Guil. Hild.)

ACT III.   SCENE II.   125

5. **Visum fuit** = *visum est.* The use of perf. part. with *fui* for *sum* is very rare in classical writers, but very frequent in Pl. So in this play III. 2. 132, *empti fuerant*, IV. 4 2, *vectus fui*, and often. See M. 344, where such forms are said to be incorrect. They may have arisen in popular speech from the feeling that the forms in *sum, eram, ero*, did not sufficiently indicate the past time of the verb. Comp. the incorrect Engl. phrase "he wanted to have gone," for "he wanted to go." See note on I. 1. 9.

8. **De prandio**, "after dinner." A very rare sense of *de* except in *diem de die*, "day after day."

9. **Clanculum**, diminutive of *clam*, found only in Pl. and Ter. "Very secretly."

13. "When I think it over further in my mind, (I conclude that) sleep," etc. A similar omission of the real leading verb occurs after *cogitare* in this scene, 101, 102. (Lor.)

15. **Neminem** = *non eum;* the negative modifies the verb and *eum* is the anteced. of quis, 14. Rit. reads *eum hominem* on conj.

15. **Sollicitat,** "tempts," "attracts" And. Lex. refers to this pass. under the meaning "to disturb, vex," which would suit Ritschl's text, but no other.

16. **Omnibus ... odio est,** "is hateful." So Men. I. 2. 2, *viro esse odio ... tibi odio.* Comp. note on *cordi*, I. 4. 10.

17. **Certa res est,** "I am determined." So Amph. II. 2. 73, and in a few other places for the much more common *certum est*, e. g., I. 3. 80.

19. **Vt moribus,** "how yours may be in character," for *quibus moribus* or *ut moratae.* (Lor.)

20. **Vostrae,** addressed to the spectators.

20. **Haec,** by its emphatic position, is put in contrast with *vostrae.* "This one — I know well enough how badly," etc. The next line depends upon *scio.*

23. **Ullum** = *quemquam. Ullus* is used as a substantive by the best writers only in gen., dat. and abl. The use of acc. as here is very rare. See M. 90, 3, obs.

24. **Merito** as an adv. (originally an abl.) is often used by class. writers with *iure*.
26. **Hoc habet!** The cry in gladiatorial games when one of the contestants received a mortal blow. Tranio's reason for using the phrase is explained in the following words.
26. **Ducerem**, in a slang use, "how I may fool the old man." *Ductare* is the more frequent word. Comp. the play upon this stem in 157, below.
27. **Dolo ... dolorem.** This Lorenz calls the only pun in the Most., because in all other places the words played upon are of the same stem. Thornton's Pl. renders, "ease myself of this disease."
30. **Quid agis?** "How do you do?" As a salutation equiv. to *ut vales*. The German Was machst du? is closer to the Latin than the English. Tran. takes the words literally and answers as if the question were "What are you doing?" Comp. II. 1. 21.
31, sq. These lines are badly mutilated in the MSS. and have been variously emended. The text is that given by Cam. The Milan palimpsest has

          .... hercle hau bonum
Teneo servom.

Simo says he does *not* have a good slave by the hand, with a hint at the bad courses of Tran. and Philol.

33. Theur. speaks this line from the side of the stage, where he is out of sight of spectators and actors. The line is removed by Rit. and placed after 52.
34-38. It must be noticed, in translating these lines, that Simo is intending to joke with Tran. by hints and innuendoes in regard to the life which he and Philol. have been leading. His sentences are therefore broken off intentionally. But beside this the MSS. are badly mutilated in 34, 35, 36, and the words in brackets are conjectures of Camerarius. The meaning is as follows: — SI. "What now? how soon (will this rioting end?)" TRAN. (pretending not to understand).

"What is it?" SI. "(I mean) what is accustomed to go on (here in your house)." TRAN. "Tell me then what you mean by 'what is accustomed to go on.'" SI. "What are you doing? But, to speak soberly, Tranio, it is fitting that as men are, you should humor them; but at the same time consider," etc.

38. **Quid.** At this point Tran. shows that he understands, and Simo breaks off his hints.

40. **Musice** = *eleganter*, with strong irony. μουσικῶς is found several times in the fragments of the New Comedy in some such sense, and this is perhaps from the original play. (Lor.)

41. **Electili**, "choice." Found only in this place. The force of *probo* and *electili* extends back to *vino* and *victu*.

42. **Imo** corrects the present tense of *co͡itis*. "No, not *now*; before this it *was* a life worth living." Comp. note on I. 4. 32, (*b*).

45. **Non taces?** Equiv. to "Don't say that!" Simo tries to comfort Tran. by refusing to believe that all is lost. On tense see 85, below.

46, sq. **Facta ... viximus.** The emphasis is upon the past time of the verbs in contrast with *nunc* of 48.

50. **Quaene** = *eamne dicis quae.* Comp. III. 1. 25. In comedy the leading clause is often omitted where it can be easily supplied from the context, and the interrogative particle is joined to the subordinate clause. Lorenz gives numerous examples. Simo, in these words, suggests that Tranio's metaphor is not applicable, because Philol. and Tran. were already safe.

51. The exclamations of Tran. are called forth by his remembrance of the difficulties in which he is involved, or possibly by some new sign of impatience on the part of Theur.

52. **Ratem**, "the oars." So Lamb. and Rit. Possibly "the hull." Various conjectures have been made to explain the use of *navi* and *ratem* in the same clause.

53. **Velim ut tu velles.** A common expression of sympathy.

Lor. quotes Sen. Ep. 67, 13, where the phrase is spoken of as in customary use. Comp. also Hor. Sat. I. ix. 5, *cupio omnia quae vis.*

54. **Chorda ... ferriterium.** A reference to the punishment of slaves. They were first bound with thongs (*chorda*), then sent to work in irons (*ferriterium*), and afterward, if further punishment was needed, they were crucified. Some reference to the last form of penalty would have followed *postea*. On the meaning of *ferriterium*, comp. *ferritribaces*, II. 1. 9.

57. **Nil moror,** "I do not care for." So frequently in Pl. Comp. Hor. Epist. I. 15, 16, II. 1. 264. *Nil* or *nihil* is the usual negative, and the verb always takes the acc. (Lor.)

58. **Hoc, quod.** The verb upon which *hoc* depends is lost by the interruption. *Quod,* acc. of "compass and extent," as often after *mitto*, M. 229, 1, or of specification.

66. **Gunaeceum,** γυναικεῖον, was the inner part of a Greek house, where the women lived. On spelling comp. *gumnastica*, I. 2. 66.

67. **Balineas.** The plu. generally refers to the public bath-houses, but here evidently to a private house, possibly, as Lor. suggests, to indicate that the apartments were to be numerous and of large size.

67. **Ambulacrum.** This was a porch in front of the house (comp. 128). Hahn (Scen. Quaest. Pl., pp. 34-37) thinks that it is only another name for the *vestibulum*.

67. **Porticum** refers to the inner porches around the *peristylium*. See Becker's Gallus or Smith's Dict. Antiq.

69. **Quantum potest** = *quam celerrime potest*, as often in Pl.

71. **Architectonem,** from nom. *architecto* or *-ton* for more common Latin form *architectus*. Found also in Poen. V. 2. 150.

72. **Esse aedificatas** depends upon the verb of saying implied in *laudasse*, which here has a sense like that in Capt. II. 3. 66, *Iovem ... testem laudo*, "I name as witness." Render, "has praised, saying that it," etc.

74-76. These verses are so incomplete in the MSS. that no thor-

ACT III. SCENE II.

oughly satisfactory text can be made. That given is from Lorenz.

74. **Nam** implies an ellipsis of some such phrase as "he is unwise," expressed perhaps by a shake of the head. Lor. very unnecessarily supposes that a line has been lost.

74. **Hinc** repeats in one word the idea of *ex malo opere*. In seeking a model from this house (*hinc*), he seeks it from a poor piece of work.

76. **Sub diu**, "under the open sky." Comp. Hor. Carm. I. 1. 25, *sub Iove*.

77. **Imo edepol vero**, "no indeed, by Pollux." Tran., knowing nothing about the house, has happened to hit upon just the wrong reason for the pretended admiration of Theur.

77. **Vsquequaque** is found again in Poen. Prol. 105, and is used by Cic. "Everywhere." *Vsque*, "all the way," "right on," "continuously." On form *mani*, 78, comp. III. 1. 3.

79. **Flagitator**, "like a dun." *Flagito* is used like *nomino*, of demanding payment by the *pipulum*. (Ram.) Comp. example quoted under III. 1. 5.

81. **Sarsinatis ... Vmbram.** A play upon the double sense of *umbra* which may mean an Umbrian woman. This line is sometimes quoted as a proof that Sarsina was the birthplace of Pl., though it is hard to find any such suggestion in the line. There is a similar coarse joke upon *Boia* in the Capt.

85. **Eon'? voco.** The pres. for the fut. is common in dialogue (A. & G. 276, *c*; G. 218, Rem. 2; H. 467, 5) to describe an action about to be commenced, particularly where a man asks himself or another what he shall do. (Roby, Lor.) This is simply an attempt at greater vividness by treating the fut. as already present, and is precisely similar to the use noticed in I. 3. 54. See also I. 1. 9, and M. 339, obs. 2, *a*.

86-94. These lines are spoken by Tran. as he goes across the stage to find Theur.

86. **Agathoclem**, the Sicilian adventurer, who held the power for 25 years from about 317 B. C.

87. **Duo.** To be taken by an unusual construction with *Alex.* and *Agath.*

87. **Mihi.** The dat. after *fieri* must be distinguished from the abl. construction. (See I. 3. 65.) Lor. compares this to the dat. after *bene (male) facere.*

89. **Vehit.** This figure, by which a person who is deceived is said to carry a load of lies, is frequent in Pl. Comp. II. 1. 82, and Engl. phrase, "to impose upon."

89. **Hic ... hic autem,** Theur. and Simo. *Autem,* "and moreover," is used in the same way, to distinguish two pronouns and to add the second to the first, in Mil. Glor. IV. 4. 13, *et illa ... et ille autem,* and in same play, III. 1. 84.

90. **Novitium ... quaestum,** "a new way of making a living."

96. The latter part of this line follows the text of Rit.

98. **Restitisti.** From *resisto; resto* in this sense, "to stop," "to linger," is very rare.

100. **Antiquom ... tuom,** sc. *morem.* "You stick to your old habit of being late." So Ter. Hec. V. 4. 20, *morem antiquom ... optines,* and without *morem,* Andr. IV. 5. 22. So Cic. Tusc. I. 42, 99, *suum illud ... tenet.* See M. 374. (Lor.) H. 495, 3.

101. **Si voles.** The apodosis is to be supplied, *scies* or *videbis.* Comp. line 13.

102. **Flare sorbereque,** "to drink and whistle," And. Lex., but it may be simply "to blow out and to draw in breath." So Lamb. takes it.

107. This line is suggested to Tran. by the desire to prevent an understanding between the old men; the plan is more fully carried out below in 121, sqq.

110. **Sibi ... metit.** A proverbial expression like "every man for himself." A similar rustic proverb occurs in Epid. II. 2. 80, *mihi istic nec seritur nec metitur,* "I have no part in it."

111. **Redhibere,** to force a defective purchase back upon the seller, while *remittat,* 109, is to give up a bargain at the request of the seller. Both words are used by the buyer. (Ram.)

112, 113. The idea is, one must keep what he gets and not let pity interfere with business.

115. **Do tibi ... operam,** "I am attending to you," "I am at your service." So IV. 4. 17, and very often in Prologues. Tran. has brought Theur. across the stage while they have been speaking 106–115, and he now performs a sort of ceremony of introduction.

119. **Flocci faxis,** often written as one word, *floccifacere*. Comp. note on I. 1. 73.

120. **Oppido** with *tamquam*, "exactly as if."

121. **Tamquam?** Theur. supposes the house to be really his own, and is surprised that Simo should say "as if it were your own." Tran. interposes to prevent an explanation. The genuine courtesy shown by Simo and Theur. suggests that these lines are from the Attic original.

123. **Admodum,** "to any (great) degree," "much."

124. **Noli facere mentionem,** "don't mention the fact that you," etc. M. 386, obs. 2; A. & G. 269, *a*; H. 535, 1, 3); G. 264, II.

126. **Quin ... is ... perspecta.** An example of *quin* with indic. and imperative without difference of meaning. See I. 3. 16, (*a*). A. & G. 269, *f*; G. 268.

127. **Bene benigneque ... facere.** A very common formula for thanks or recognition of kindness. Render, "You are very kind and obliging, I'm sure."

127. **Factum ... volo,** "I want to be," or "I do so willingly."

After 127 the MSS. have two lines which are repeated with slight variation in 157–8, and are therefore omitted here by most editors.

129. **Luculentum** is taken in the literal sense by And. Lex., but this sense is rare, and the usual meaning agrees better with the context. "Fine, splendid."

131. **Non videor vidisse,** sc. *mihi*, "I do not think I have seen." Comp. the same words in I. 3. 113.

132. **Empti fuerant.** On *fuerant* for *erant*, see III. 2. 5. It has been noticed under I. 3. 54, that the plupf. is sometimes used

for the perf., but here the reason given does not seem applicable. The plupf. seems to be used in order to give an opportunity for Tranio's comment, "Did you hear him say they *had* been, as if they were no longer his?" In 134 Simo uses the perf. *dedi* of the same transaction, but in 132 Theur. says *emeras* because he believes that the house no longer belongs to Simo.

133. **Vix .. lacrumas.** Lor. suggests that Simo may have spoken the words *Pol . . . olim* with a mournful shake of the head, as a man might speak of his past extravagance.

135. **Multum,** for abl. of degree of difference. See M. 270, obs. 1; H. 418, 1; G. 400, 2.

137. **Intempestivos.** Winter was the proper season for felling timber, and wood cut at another time was liable to decay.

138. **Atque,** "and yet." So Trin. II. 2. 55, *qui . . . nusquam . . . rem confregit, atque eget,* " never used up his property, and yet is in want." So Men. IV. 2. 2. (Hild. Wag.)

139. **Pultiphagus opifex . . . barbarus.** The food of the Roman lower classes was a porridge made of *far*, and called *puls* or *pulmentum*. *Pultiphagus* or *pultifagus* therefore refers to the Romans. It is from *puls* and the stem φαγ-, or as Rost says, from πόλτος and φαγ-. Pl. often places himself in the position of a Greek and calls the Romans *barbari*, both to raise a laugh and to satisfy the police censors by keeping some Greek tone in the play. See Intro. (Ram. Lamb. See also Rost. Opusc. I. pp. 247–252.)

140. **Dormiunt.** A comic use of the word, which Tran. is obliged to explain to Theur. *Conivent (connivent)*, which is offered as an explanation, is used in the same comic way, with even greater departure from the original sense, "to wink." The idea of both here is "to rest securely."

142. **Satin' habes?** "Now do you get the idea?"

142. **Quicquid** for *quicque*, as often in the comic writers. M. 495, obs. 1, end.

143. **Cornix, volturios.** The *cornix* is the common type of a cunning and crafty fellow, and the *volturius* of a rapacious man.

ACT III.   SCENE II.   133

There is, of course, no such picture on the wall, and Tran., in exultation over his success, is playing upon the easy credulity of Theur. (Lor.)

146. **Huc ad me.** While Tran. says and means *ad me*, he points to a place on the wall near himself. So *isto ad vos*, 148.

147. **Intuor.** On the two forms of this verb in Pl. see note on I. 1. 66, and comp. below 148, 149, 152.

149. **Si ... possis.** *Si* in indirect questions is especially frequent with *possim*. M. 451, *d*. "After verbs implying trial," G. 462, 2.

151. **Vt te apsolvam,** "to get rid of you." So Aul. III. 5. 43, *apsolutos*, "dismissed."

152. **Mitto,** "I let you off." So in V. 3. 50. *Aetate*, "because of your age," i. e., you are too old to see clearly.

153. **Quae possum,** sc. *optueri*. *Ea* is a repetition of *haec*, because of the intervening clause.

154. **Operae pretium,** "it is worth while," "worth the trouble." Very frequent in Pl., e. g., Poen. V. 4. 1, Rud. IV. 3. 10, and with ellipsis of *pretium*, Merc. V. 2. 77, *operae non est*.

154. **Ivisse** for *ire*, the act being thought of as already finished.

155. **Circumduce,** with two acc. So Caes. B. C. III. 61.

158. **Quidquid est,** "in any case." *Perductet* is taken by Theur. in a frequent comic sense, "to cheat," and the next words of Simo explain that he had no such thought in his mind.

160. **Canis.** The custom of keeping a dog at the door of the house was general in early times of the Republic. Later the dog was represented by a figure in the mosaic of the entrance.

164. **Bene ambula.** So Cas. III. 1. 12, Pers. I. 1. 51, etc. A common formula of farewell. "A pleasant walk to you!" *Bon voyage*. Simo goes out toward the city.

168. After this line Tran. and Theur. go into the house, and the stage is left vacant for a moment or two.

ACT IV. SCENE I.

Phaniscus comes upon the stage alone, going toward the house of Philolaches to escort Callidamates home according to his order, I. 4. 1. The first 25 lines are the third *canticum*.

The lines of this scene will be found to be very different in different editions, according to the metrical theories of the editors. Hermann, Ritschl, and Weise have arrangements differing widely from each other; the last in particular "distributes the forty-two lines into fifty-eight," in the course of which he supposes the metre to change thirty times. (See Ram. Prol. p. 52.)

1. A passage almost precisely similar to this is found in Men. V. 6. 22.
1. **Carint** = *careant*. M. 115, *d*; H. 239, 3; G. 191, 3, says that such forms "seem to be doubtful." Lorenz reads *carent* on the ground that the idea of time is stronger than that of concession.
1. **Malum**, "punishment," a frequent meaning in Pl.
2. **Vtibiles** = *utiles*. The ending *–bilis* is synonymous with *–lis*, and seems to be the older. *Vtibilis* is used six times by Pl. See M. 185, 2, *a* & *b*; A. & G. 164, *m*; H. 328, 3; G. 786, 6.
3. **Nihil metuont**, i. e., have no fear sufficient to deter them from folly which will bring punishment.
6. **Peculium**, the property which a slave holds as his own. The sense of the passage is:—These slaves, when they have committed a fault, add to it by running away. So when they are caught, they find that they have laid up a store of punishment for themselves, a sort of hoard of evil, though they are too lazy to lay up a store of good things.
7. **Inde**, i. e., from the *peculium*. "They make a treasure out of it."
8. **Mihi ... quod est.** Comp. the omission of leading clause in III. 2. 13, 101. The text of Rit. is somewhat simpler for this line.

> Mihi in pectore [id] consili[st, praecavere].

9. **Quam ut.** *Vt* is used with *quam* in prose after *ante, prius* and

ACT IV. SCENE I. 135

citius, to denote "what is to be warded off at any cost." (Lor.) Comp. M. 360, obs. 4; A & G. 332, *b*; H. 496, 2; G. 313, "*Disproportion* is expressed by the comparative with *quam ut*." So *facilius quam ut*, V. 3. 48, sq.

11. **Sincerum**, "uncut by the scourge." In the same sense, Rud. III. 4. 52.

11. **Atque ut** = *atque tale ut*. *Votem* = *vetem*. The sense is somewhat doubtful. Render, "My skin ought to be whole, as it has been hitherto, and such that I may forbid (not allow) it to be beaten. If I shall give this command to it, I shall have it very well protected." *Votem* means "I may forbid by obedience to my master," and *imperabo* carries out the same thought.

13. **Inpluit.** Comp. *perpluont*, I. 2. 27. And. Lex. gives examples of both personal and impersonal uses, and of acc. and dat. as in this line.

15. The reading of Lor. is followed here. *Boni sunt* is a hypothesis, with almost the force of a question or condition.

16. **Nam.** Supply a clause from *malus fit*. "(So our master will be) for," etc.

17. **Peculi** may be taken literally, but better figuratively for their backs, their only possession. There is no reference to lines 6–7. For gen. see M. 290, *e*, obs. 2; A. & G. 218, *a*; G. 373; H. 399, 2.

17. **Plagigeruli** is found in no other place, though *plagiger* occurs in Pseud. I. 2. 20. Both words were probably coined by Pl.

17. **Advorsum ... eant.** These words give the name Advorsitor to Phan. and to the other slave who comes in later. See list of Dram. Pers.

19. **Gestis aliquo**, sc. *ire*. *Gestio* is rarely used absolutely. These two lines are the excuses presented by the other slaves, insinuating that Phan. is going to some cook-shop or drinking-saloon.

19. **Mula**, the type of voracity with the Romans.

20. **Bene merens** = *dum bene mereo*. (Lamb.) "For my obedience." *Inde* = *ab iis*. Comp. *unde* = *a quo*, III. 1. 16.

22. **Die crastini.** The phrases *die quarti* or *quarte, quinti, septimi, noni, pristini*, etc., were considered adverbial by the grammarians (Aul. Gell. X, 24), but it is almost certain that they were locatives. The locative of the 5th decl. ends in *e*, of the 2d in *i*. Comp. 3d decl. locatives of time, *vesperi, temperi, mani.*

23. **Bubulis exuviis,** lashes of oxhide, which would properly be called *exuviae*. The phrase had doubtless a comic sound to a Roman ear.

24. **Postremo,** "in short," as in I. 3. 41. Ram. renders, "Well, well, at all events."

25. **Bucaedae** (*bos* + *caedo*) is found only in this passage, and is probably one of the numerous words coined by Pl. to describe punishments. By its composition it should be active in meaning, as is *restio*, but both words are used for comic effect with passive sense. Render, "they shall have oxhide cuttings, rather than that I should have dealings with ropes." *Restio* refers either to flogging with cords or to binding for scourging. So Pers. II. 4. 11, *caedere hodie tu restibus.*

26. At this point another slave of Call. comes upon the stage on the same errand as Phaniscus. He is called indifferently Servos Alius or Advorsitor. The Vulgate make a new scene here.

28. **Simia** is often used as a term of reproach, without any special reference. Here it may be, as And. Lex. says, a hint that Phan. is trying to imitate his master.

28. **Mihi sum,** "I am so for myself," i.e., "that is *my* affair," not yours.

29. **Manesne.** Pres. for fut. as in III. 2. 85. *Ne* with the force of *nonne* as in III. 1. 125. "Are you going to stop?" "Won't you stop?"

31. **Ferocem facis,** "you play the bully," like Engl. "play the fool," Germ. "Du spielst (giebst) den stolzen," Fr. "faire le brave." So Curc. IV. 3. 7, *facias ferocem.* (Taub.)

32. Lamb. and Taub. say that the wit of this line is in the unexpected literalness of the answer. Lorenz explains as fol-

lows: *Oculi dolent* is a general phrase expressive of disgust or annoyance. So Ter. Phorm. V. 9. 64. *Fumus* is a translation of καπνός, which is used by Plato and Aristoph. to mean "nonsense." Comp. *fumum vendere*, "to make empty promises." The words would then be an expression of annoyance at being stopped to listen to nonsense.

33. **Faber,** etc., a counterfeiter. He means that Phan. is accustomed to pass himself off upon his master as a good slave, while in fact he is not so.

36. **Si ... sis .. dicas,** for *si esses, diceres*. Comp. III. 1. 24, and note.

39. **Maxumam ... iniuriam.** Similar scenes of violent knocking are common, e.g., Stich. II. 1. 39 sq. Bacch. IV. 2. 2 sq. Comp. also II. 2. 23, 25. For the dat. *foribus*, comp. Virg. Ecl. VII. 47, *solstitium pecori defendere*, and examples in And. Lex. under *defendo*. A. & G. 229; H. 386, 2; M. 243; G. 344, 2.

41. **Vt .. sunt.** "As it is natural for worthless men to be, so these are," because they do not answer.

42. **Eo,** i. e., because they are worthless, and likely to be reckless if they are angry.

42. **Cauto opus est.** *Cauto* is abl. neut. of the partic. Instead of the infinitive after *opus est*, "the abl. of a participle, or substantive combined with a participle, is often employed." M. 266 obs. See H. 419, V. 3. 1); A. & G. 292, *b*; G. 390. Comp. Liv. I. 58, *opus est maturato*, Trin. II. 4. 183, *quid opus facto*. The partic. may take the case of the verb, as in the last example.

42. **Male mulcet,** "soothe me unpleasantly," "stroke me the wrong way."

After this line the slaves retire from the door and stand in the vestibulum, where they are not in sight from the door or from Simo's house.

ACT IV. SCENE II.

Theuropides and Tranio come out of the house of Simo, and stand near the door till the end of the scene.

1. **Quid** = *quale*. "What sort of a bargain?"
3. **Abiectas**, "thrown away," i. e., sold for too small a price.
4. **Imo.** See I. 4. 22 (*b*). It corrects the inadequate expression in *ecquid*. "No indeed, by Hercules (not 'at all,' as you say; that is not strong enough), it pleases me *altogether*" (*perplacent*). Comp. IV. 4. 38, and Ter. Eun. IV. 7. 42, *Credin'?* G. *Imo certe, novi ingenium,* "Do you think so?" G. "(Think so!) No, not at all, ('think' is too weak a word) I *know*," etc.
5. **Insanum** is evidently a slang phrase, like the exaggerated use of "awful," "immense." Comp. Mil. Glor. I. 1. 24, *esuriem insane bene*, spoken by a hungry parasite.
7. **Quin** introduces a statement to strengthen *existumo*. "Why, I tell you, we have measured." The lie is of course invented on the spur of the moment, without any real necessity for it.
9. **Mercimoni lepidi.** Lorenz calls this the very uncommon gen. in exclamations, and comp. Prop. IV. 7. 21, *foederis heu taciti*, and Lucan II. 45, *o miserae sortis*. The construction does not seem to be noticed in the American grammars nor in Roby.
13. **Audacter dicito,** "boldly," i. e., without fear of contradiction.
15. **Isti**, Simo, who is referred to by *huic*, 16, by *illi*, 18, and without a pron. is the subj. of *accipiat*, 17. This is a good illustration of the freedom of Pl. in the use of pronouns.
16. **Octaginta.** The price was two talents, 120 minae, of which 40 were supposed to have been paid as *arrabo*.
17. **Ne qua causa**, i. e., any cause for delay or hesitation on the part of Simo. Tran. really wishes to get hold of the money.
18. **Porro,** "then," "in turn."
19. **At enim** indicates a refusal. Comp. III. 1. 20, *nihil enim*, and V. 3. 23. So below, line 23, "No, for I have," etc.

19. **Ne quid ... sit,** sc. *metuo.* The ellipsis is frequent; it occurs in Stich. IV. 2. 20, Pseud. I. 5. 22, and elsewhere. (Lor.) *Captioni,* dat. of end or purpose, or predicative dat. (Roby); comp. *cordi,* I. 4. 10. *Captio* may well enough be taken in its original sense, "a snare," "a fraud," not as in And. Lex.
20. **Modo** goes with *ioculo,* "in jest even." Notice the indignation expressed by *–ne* appended to *ego.*
21. **Aps te ... cavere.** So Men. I. 2. 42, *aps te caveo,* Men. II. 1. 41, *aps te metuo,* and frequently after verbs of caution or fear. Plautus in several places makes his old men brag of their watchfulness just when they are most deceived, e. g., Capt. II. 2. 5 sqq.
22. **Quia.** The leading verb is omitted. "Do you say that, because," etc.
24. **Sat sapio.** The meaning is, I am showing wisdom enough if I succeed in avoiding your tricks. Tranio's answer has a double sense, because the spectators know that he is really deceiving Theur. while he speaks.
25. **Rus.** This evidently implies a statement from Tran. that Philol. had gone out to the country-seat, from which Grumio came in the first scene. No such statement appears in the play, however; it may have been lost, or the discrepancy may have been overlooked by Pl.
27. **Posticum.** The back-door of the Roman house, opening from the garden into a side-street, through which Tran. could enter unseen by Theur.
27. **Congerrones.** A word of doubtful etymol. and meaning. Ram. seems to refer it to *gerrae,* "nonsense," making it mean "companions in trifling." Rost. (Opusc. I. 280–284) makes it the same as *congerones,* "thieves." The definition in And. Lex. will suit all passages. The word is not found out of Pl., except in the grammarians.

ACT IV. SCENE III.

Phaniscus and the other Advorsitor come out from the vestibulum, and continue their attempts to enter the house of Philolaches. They are now for the first time noticed by Theuropides, who had before been occupied with Tranio.

2. **Tibicinam.** Flute-girls, who sometimes danced while playing, were introduced at feasts to amuse the guests. Comp. Xen. Symp. II. 1. *Canto* is the reg. verb for playing upon the *tibia*. Comp. *tibicen* (*tibia* + *cano*).

3. **Illio**, the adv. But two good MSS. give *illisce*, which may be the correct reading. Comp. II. 2. 77.

4. **Introspectant.** Becker suggests that this may refer to looking in at the windows, which in that case must have been low. But it is unusual in a Roman house to find any windows toward the street. It may perhaps refer to looking through the key-hole, which was a large aperture in the door. It must be noticed that these slaves do not seem to observe that the house has been locked from without by the *clavis Laconica*.

5. **Fabula** means their knocking at a house which Theur. supposes to have been closed for six months. The same phrase occurs in Ter. Andr. IV. 4. 8, where Colman translates, "What farce is this?"

7. After this line the Milan Palimpsest gives six lines which are not found in any other MS., but the writing is so faint that only a few words can be made out.

9. **Puere**, voc. from the orig. form *puerus*.

9. **Nimium delicatus es,** "you are too much of a joker." This sense of *delicatus* is rare, and is not given in And. Lex. So, possibly, in Rud. II. 5. 8. Comp. the common phrase *delicias facere*, "to joke." (Taub. Ram) Lor. compares τρυφάω, which has two meanings corresponding to those of *delicatus*.

11. **Nam,** "I give you this explanation, for," etc. *Probrum*, because of his respectful manner, which appears throughout the dialogue.

ACT IV.   SCENE III.   141

12. After this line the Palimpsest gives another which is thus restored by Rit. The italics are conjectural letters: —

    Habitavit: verum *emigravit pridem ille ex* hisce aedibus.

    The line is spoken by Theur.
13. **Pervorse** has no suggestion of wilfulness like the Engl. words from the same stem.
17. **Nudiustertius** = *nunc* + *dius* (*dies*) + *tertius*, "it is now the third day," "day before yesterday."
19. **Triduom unum,** "a single space of three days." *Vnum* is emphatic, not for indef. article. *Desitum est* is impersonal pass., and so *intermissum est* in next line.
20. The reading of the MSS. has been retained here, though there is an unpleasant confusion of act. and pass. infinitives. *Pergraecari* may best be taken as a depon.
25. **Quisquis est.** Theur. wishes to seem to be a stranger, until he has discovered the truth.
26. **Praeter speciem,** i. e., beyond what one would expect from so pleasant a slave.
27. **Merendam,** a luncheon taken at noon or soon after. It is considered by Becker (Gallus, p. 455) the same as the *prandium*, which came at twelve or one o'clock. So Smith's Dict. Antiq. p. 306, *b*. And. Lex. says "between four and five," which is too late in the day.
27. **Quopiam,** to some cook-shop, where the Romans of the lower classes took luncheon, and where a mixture of wine and honey with hot water was sold with the luncheon.
29. **Alias,** to some other house, as you have come here by mistake.
34. **Μὰ τὸν Ἀπόλλω.** The slave has multiplied the amount by sixty in saying *talentis,* and Phan. corrects him with an oath at the exaggeration.
36. **Manu emisisse.** The regular Plautine phrase, for which later usage has *manumitto.* Comp. Arg. line 1, with note.
39. **Huic,** Simo. By some referred to the house, but without necessity, since the freedom of Pl. in the use of pronouns accounts for the absence of the antecedent.

40. **Imo** corrects the subject and the implied object of *perdis*. "No, *I* am not destroying *you*," etc. See I. 4. 22, (*b*).
42. The sense is, "by what you reveal, you proclaim that that father is a wretched man."
43. **Prae quam**, "in comparison with," "compared with the fact that." So V. 3. 25, and Amph. II. 2. 3. *Prae quod* and *prae ut* are used by Pl. in the same sense. (Ram.)
44. **Vnus ... sacerrumus**, "a cursed scoundrel." (Ram.) For *unus* with the force of the indef. article see III. 1. 142.
45. **Herculi conterere quaestum**. Hercules was looked upon as the guardian of the treasures hidden in the earth; *quaestum* may refer also to the sums which he received from the practice of dedicating a tenth to him by sumptuous public banquets. In 46, *ne = nae*.
47. **Corculum carbunculus**. These diminutives do not differ in meaning from the simple forms, and are used merely for the half-comic jingle of sound.
48. **Merear**, "gain." Comp. *meruerunt*, "have bought," I. 3. 124.
50. After this line the traces of another appear in the Palimpsest as follows: —

    Puere .... q .... hacme ....

Rit. supposes that the line contained a request from Theur. that Phan. would follow him and confront Tran., and that Phan. refused, and proposed to leave, explaining that he was not at liberty to go where he pleased. The text follows Rit. from 49 to the end in the assignment of the dialogue to the different characters.

ACT IV. SCENE IV.

The slaves go away to look for Callidamates, and Theuropides speaks the first four lines before he sees Simo, who is returning from the forum.

1. **Vt verba audio**, "as far as I can hear," "judging by what I hear." Comp. Pseud. I. 1. 97, *ut sermonem audio*. (Lor.)

ACT IV.   SCENE IV.   143

3. **Terras solas,** "solitudes." So Aul. IV. 6. 7, *solum locum*, and Rud. IV. 4. 141, *solo loco*. (Lamb.)
4. **Ita**, absolutely as in I. 2. 61, and often.
5. **Scibo** = *sciam*. Comp. I. 3. 59, and see G. 191, 1; M. 115, *c*; A. & G. 128, *e*, 1; H. 239, 1.
6. **Quid agis tu?** As in II. 1. 21, and III. 2. 30, a joke is attempted by giving a literal answer to this question, instead of returning some general form of salutation. The same vein of joking runs through the following lines; Theur. is anxious about his affairs, and asks questions almost at random, trying to appear unconcerned, while Simo is mindful of his promise to Tran. in III. 2. 56, and rather inclined to be jolly.
7. **Processit,** "has anything happened?" *Ad forum*, comp. *ad portum*, II. 1. 5.
8. **Etiam,** "yes." M. 454; H. 346, II. 3; A. & G. 212, *a*; G. 473, 1. The answer is intended to be unsatisfactory.
9. **Novom,** "news, indeed!"
10. **Modo ... aiebant.** The words are of course absurd and intentionally pointless.
10. **Vae capiti tuo,** "confound you!" On this use of *caput*, comp. I. 3. 54. " This is a formula employed when a speaker feels disgusted at being made the object of an ill-timed jest." (Ram.) It is very common in Pl. and Ter.
11. **Otiosus,** "like an idler." Simo suggests the reason which justifies his impertinence.
12. **Promisi foras,** etc. It was a Greek custom to invite a friend to supper on the first night after his return from abroad. Simo pretends to think that Theur. is seeking such an invitation, and gives his excuse for not offering it. On *foras*, see I. 1. 1. Either *foras* or *foris* may be used in this connection, according to the prominence given to the idea of motion. Stich. IV. 2. 16, *ad cenam ... promisi foris*. Simo's offer to dine with Theur. if he does not get some other invitation, is pure impertinence.
17. **Maxume,** "gladly." So V. 3. 23, and often.

20. **Multo ... minus,** "much less have I received any money from Tranio, who would be the last man to pay his debts."
23. **Potesse** = *posse.* See note on *pote*, I. 3. 99.
24. **Quid, quod.** Both words refer to *hoc.*
25. **Vt ... gesserit.** "An impossible supposition put interrogatively." (Roby.) This use of *ut* is nearly confined to comedy, and is not noticed in And. Lex. It perhaps arose from an ellipsis of some such phrase as "Is it likely?" "Is it possible?" Men. IV. 3. 9, *mihi ut tu dederis pallam?* "Is it likely that you gave?" Truc. II. 4. 87, *egone illam ut non amem?* "Is it possible that I should not love her?" Comp. the rhetorical questions in Cic. Cat. I. 9. *Te ut ulla res frangat?* etc. (Ram. Excurs. IX.) See M. 353, obs.; G. 560.
29. **Ire infitias,** "to deny." *Infitias* is an acc. of limit of motion, used only with *ire*. From *in* (neg.) and *fateor*. So Men. II. 3. 45, V. 8. 8. Sometimes taken from *in* + *facio* and spelled *inficias*, but with less authority. Comp. *suppetias ire*, "to help." (Hild.)
31. **Hinc,** from Philolaches.
33. **Aiebat,** sc. Tranio. Because of the omission of the subject, the lack of explanation between Simo and Theur., the omission of *aedibus* after *tuis*, 34, and some reasons drawn from the condition of the Palimpsest, Ritschl supplies 23 lines between 32 and 33.
38. **Imo** corrects the negative implied in *numquid*, and the inadequate expression in *quid* and *turbavit*, putting in *omnia* and *exturbavit*. See I. 4. 22, (*c*). *Exturbare* is used of expelling a man from his house. Lor. renders the two verbs by *gespielt* and *verspielt*.
43. **Mecum una simul.** This pleonasm occurs in Poen. III. 1. 50, Pseud. I. 4. 17. (Lor.)
45. **Eadem opera,** originally "with the same effort" or "during the same action," but often as here, "at the same time." Comp. *una opera*, I. 3. 102.

After line 46 the two old men go into Simo's house, and the stage is left vacant for the second time.

ACT V. SCENE I.

The following scene is not a *canticum*, but is spoken by Tranio himself, who comes on the stage as if from the country.

1. **Nauci.** The construction is like that of *nihili*, I. 2. 70. Except in one pass. it always has a neg. with it. Brix (Trin. 396) suggests that *nauci* may be connected with *nugae*, through the form *naugae*, which is given by some MSS.
3. **Nam** introduces an explanation, as in Amph. Prol. 104, Truc. IV. 4. 3, where some general phrase may be supplied. "I am led to make this remark, for," etc. There is no need of supposing that a line has dropped out, as Rit. and Lor. often do. (See Ram. Excurs. VI.)
4. **Angiportum**, a narrow lane between two blocks of houses, as in Pseud. IV. 2. 6, or a private passage-way between two houses, as here. Such a passage, leading from a side street to the garden, may be seen in the plan of the "House of the Tragic Poet," in Becker's Gallus or Smith's Dict. Antiq.
5. **Ostium quod** = *quod ostium*. (M. 319.) Supply *eius* as anteced., depending on *fores*. *Ostium* is the doorway; *fores* are the doors by which the doorway is closed. Connect *horti* with *angiportu*.
9. **Quom ... atque,** "when ... at once." Comp. Epid. II. 2. 33, *quom venio, atque ego video*, "when I come, at once I see," etc. So also *ut ... atque*. Comp. analogous uses of *atque* in II. 2. 57, and III. 2. 138.
10. **Vorti ... in meo foro,** "that the matter is referred to my court;" strictly "is carried on in my court," spoken as if he were the presiding judge. The more common explanation, which makes Tran. put himself in the position of the accused, is incorrect. (See Rost, p. 137.)
    On the sentiment of the following lines comp. III. 1. 15. The same figure of disturbed wine has been used in II. 1. 68.
13. **Clam senem.** *Clam* is used only once or twice as a prepos.

in class. prose, but is very common in Pl. and Ter. with acc. and is found rarely with abl.

After this line the Palimpsest shows traces of seven lines, of which only three broken words can be deciphered.

14. **Vicinia**, abl., abstract for concrete. It refers to Simo's house.

ACT V. SCENE II.

Theuropides comes out of Simo's house, leaving the *lorarii* (see IV. 4. 44) concealed just within the door. While he is still busy with arranging his plan, Tranio comes near and overhears the first words of the scene.

1. Notice the repetition of words of place in *ilico, intra limen, illic*, and of advs. of time in *quom, extemplo, continuo*. These two lines are addressed to the *lorarii*.
4. **Ludificabor** is used with ironical reference to *ludificatorem*.
5. **Res palam est.** Tran. hears the words and understands at once that his tricks are known.
6. **Captandum est cum illo**, an unusual phrase nearly equiv. to *captandus est ille*. Comp. V. 3. 21, *tecum cavendum est*.
7. The reading of Lorenz is followed here; it is decidedly better than Rit. or Ram.
8. **Malum**, "cunning, dangerous." Comp. δεινός. (Lor.)
10. **Lapidi**, a type of stupidity, like *saxum*. After giving Theur. ironical praise in the preceding lines, Tran. unexpectedly speaks the plain truth. This is the figure called παρὰ προσδοκίαν.
12. **Praesens praesenti.** Comp. Pseud. IV. 7. 43, *praesens praesentem videt*, Virg. Aen. IV. 83, *illum absens absentem auditque videtque*.
13. **Ruri**, "from the country." *Rure* is commonly used in this sense, and *ruri* (locative) means "in the country." But the two forms were often interchanged. So Truc. III. 2. 1, *ruri redire*, Truc. III. 2. 25, *ruri venire*, both for *rure*.
16. **Qui** = *quom is*, "inasmuch as he," "in that he." Bothe reads *quia*. Simo had not denied all knowledge of Tran., but

ACT V. SCENE II. 147

Theur. exaggerates in order to make an answer more difficult for Tran.

23. **Istuc idem.** These words may refer to the preceding line, "I said that he had sold the house, and taken part of the money for it." Acidal. and Rit. suppose that a line has fallen out.

24. **Quaestioni,** an examination by torture on the rack, *equuleus*. The practice was common among both Greeks and Romans. Theur. tells this lie in order to get a pretence for bringing out the *lorarii*, as if they were to be examined.

24. **Nugas,** sc. *agit*, and comp. the use of *nugas agis* in Men. IV. 2. 57 sqq.

25. **Mane.** Tranio wishes to get away, and after his last words starts as if he were going to find Simo. Ritschl recasts the line thus : —

   Quin cita illum in ius. ibo, inveniam,

   in order to account the better for *mane*. In the following words Theur. at first says that he thinks he will try the plan, and then, as he sees Tran. still inclined to go, he goes further and says that he is determined to do it.

26. **Cedo,** i. e., bring him to me, hand him over to me to settle the matter.

28. **Mancupio.** See And. Lex. and Smith's Dict. Antiq. As this method of transferring property could only be used by one who had a full title, *mancupio dare* (*accipere*) may be rendered " with a full title," the usual sense in Pl. But *poscere mancupio* could only be used of the purchaser; we must therefore either make *hominem* refer to Philol., or make it the second object of *poscere*, or suppose that Pl. has confused the legal terms. Ramsay prefers the second explanation, Lorenz and Rost the third, which on the whole seems the most satisfactory.

30. **Hanc aram.** See Introduction to Most.

31. **Enim.** "You don't understand the matter; for (I take possession of the altar) that they may not be able," etc.

32. **Interbitat** = *intereat*. Found only here. The simple verb

beto is used four times by Pl., always in the sense of *eo*. (Lor.)

35. **Argenti**, gen. analogous to gen. of crime after verbs of accusing, etc. The fact that the slaves attempted to escape the *quaestio* would suggest that they had something to conceal.

36. **Quod agis, id agas**, "attend to what you are doing," to the obtaining of evidence from the slaves. Lor. compares Ter. Andr. I. 2. 15, *hocine agis, annon?* Mil. Glor. II. 2. 60, *age, si quid agis,* and the formula *hoc age*, " attend to this," used to command silence in sacrifices.

37. **Meticulosa**, "full of fear." Here in active sense "causing fear." In Amph. I. 1. 137, it is passive. Not found elsewhere in Pl., or in any class. writer. (Ram.)

38. **Igitur**, "then," i. e., when you have risen and come hither. Comp. note on I. 2. 47.

41. **Contra**, an adv., "in the face." The ordinary use in Pl. (Lor.) In only two cases in Pl. *contra* has the force of a prepos.

41. **Vides**. Theur. gives up the attempt to deceive Tran., and lets his anger appear in his face.

43. **Siet**. *Ita* must be supplied in the second clause; it is placed in the text by Rit., who has *sit ei, ita*. The sense is, "we are both so sharp (*mali*), that no third person who tried to come into this affair would be able to make enough to keep himself from starving."

45. **Med** = *me*. Comp. *ted*, II. 1. 18. Render, "you have completely cheated me."

48. **Eradicitus** is not found elsewhere except in a quotation of this passage, and was probably coined by Pl. *Radicitus* means "down to the roots;" *eradicitus* suggests, " I have pulled them up by the roots."

49. **Destinaveris**, "shall you have fixed," "concocted." Comp. use in III. 1. 110.

50. **Sarmen**, for *sarmentum*, is found only here. Comp. *vimen, vimentum*. It would not be allowable to tear Tran. from the altar by violence, but he might be driven off by fire. The same plan is proposed in Rud. III. 4. 56.

ACT V.   SCENE III.   149

52. **Exempla, exemplum.** "Example" is used in the same two senses in Engl., for warning or for imitation. From the original meaning, *exempla facere (edere) in aliquem* comes to mean "to torture." So Caes. joins it with *cruciatus*. (Lor.)

55. **Aliud**, in the first case, "different from your answer;" in the second, "different from your question."

ACT V.   SCENE III.

Tranio remains seated upon the altar. Callidamates comes in from the city, and speaks the first seven lines while he walks across the stage toward the house of Simo.

1. **Somnum sepelivi** is unusual. "When I finished all my sleep." Translatio est a sepultis, qui iam nulli sunt; somnus igitur sepultus, nullus est. (Lamb.)

5. **De sodalitate,** "of his friends." Comp. similar use of Engl. "acquaintance."

5. **Orator,** in double sense of ambassador and beseecher. Comp. note on *oro*, III. 1. 147. So also in Stich. III. 2. 34, 39, where a pun is made upon the double meaning.

8. **Hic ... cenes.** This is in accordance with the custom referred to in IV. 4. 12.

8. **Sic face** (*fac*) seems to have been a part of the formal invitation to dinner. Comp. Stich. I. 3. 31, *veni illo ad cenam: sic face*, where the words are given as the common form of invitation.

9. **Facio gratiam,** a polite way of declining the invitation. "I am much obliged, (but must be excused.)" So Men. II. 3. 36, *bene vocas; tam gratia*, "you are very kind to ask me, (but I cannot come;) I am just as much obliged." So Stich. III. 2. 18. Comp. *benigne* as a form of refusal, Hor. Epist. I. 7. 62, I. 5. 16. (Hild. Ram.) Greek ἐπαινῶ, κάλλιστα.

11. **Quian'.** The leading clause is to be supplied. "Do you say I am laughing at you, because," etc. So III. 1. 25, III. 2. 50.

12. **Ferare faxo,** sc. *ut*. See note on I. 1. 65.

13. **Ad me ad cenam.** A common repetition in Pl., found in

Stich. IV. 1. 6, and III. 2. 30. So Mil. Glor. III. 1. 118, *ad se ad prandium*. (Lor.)

14. **Inscitissumus,** "you stupid fellow." Nom. for voc.
16. **Disputa,** "tell, relate." So in Men. Prol. 50.
21. **Nimis** with *catus*, "very shrewd." *Qui es*, "since you are." Comp. *qui negat*, V. 2. 16.
22. **Sine ... dum.** Tmesis. So in Men. II. 3. 27. Lor. has a number of examples of tmesis in Pl.
23. **Enim,** "no, for there is a trick in this." Rit. gives the whole line to Tran., as if he surrendered his seat.
24. **Vicem.** See note on II. 1. 8. The sense is: Before I give up my seat, you must relieve me from all fear, and must take the consequences upon yourself.
27. **Sapere,** sc. *eos*, as subject, and anteced. of *qui*.
30. **Frustrationes,** lit. "tricks." "You will serve in the comedies as a subject for fine displays of cheating." Comp. original sense of *frustra*, III. 1. 36. Old men, who are cajoled and cheated, are a stock subject in the New Comedy, and in Pl. and Ter.
32. **Gnato tuo.** The dat. is frequent in Pl. and Ter. for gen. with a noun in the predicate, to indicate the relation in which one person stands to another. So Mil. Glor. II. 2. 116, *illic est Philocomasio custos*. So *matrem (patrem) esse alicui*. (Lor.)
33. **Is ... illum,** Philol. Comp. IV. 2. 15, and note.
40. **Inpetrabilis,** active in meaning, as in Merc. III. 4. 20, Epid. III. 2. 6, but passive in Livy. So *vincibilis, placabilis*, act. in Ter., but pass. in class. writers. M. 185, 2, *b*, obs. 1. (Lor.) H. 328, 3; G. 786, 6.
41. **Sum iratus ... suscenseo.** There is no distinction of meaning between these words. Their use together is only another manifestation of the tautology natural to conversation. (Lor.)
45. **Lutum,** a term of reproach, used also in Pers. III. 3. 2, 10. So *caenum* and *inluvies*. In such expressions, as in terms of endearment, the vocabulary of Plautus is very rich. *Caedere*, fut. pass. 2d sing.

45. **Pendens.** Slaves were sometimes suspended by the hands with weights attached to the feet, and flogged in that position.

46. **Cunctam,** "including all," "general." *Pessum* (from *pes, pedis*) is used by Pl. and Ter. with *ire, dare,* and some other verbs of motion. It is called by Roby an acc. of limit of motion, and may be rendered "to destruction." Or *pessum dare* (*agere, premere*) may be rendered "to destroy."

50. **Restat,** "resists," a rare sense. So Ter. Heaut. V. 3. 7.

55. The text of this line is from Ritschl.

56. **Commeream,** "commit," a meaning easily derived from the original one, and common in Pl. and Ter. So in this play, II. 2. 83; in Merc. IV. 6. 12, *culpam commerent,* "commit a fault."

59. **Cantor.** This was the singer, who stood by the flute-player, and chanted the words of the *cantica*. This person speaks the last words of appeal to the audience in several of the comedies. (Amph., Truc., Pers.) In several plays he speaks only the word *plaudite* (Rud., Mil. Glor.). Sometimes these words were given by the whole company, *Grex* or *Caterva* (Cist., Capt.), and possibly in the Epid. they were spoken by Plautus himself. (Lor.)

EDITIONS OF PLAUTUS.

The following partial list of editions is added for the convenience of any who may wish to make a thorough study of Plautus. A full bibliography up to the year 1829 is given in Valpy's reprint of the Delphin edition: —

1605. Lambinus.
1621. Text by Gruter, notes by Taubmann.
1669. Variorum. (Vulgate.) J. F. Gronovius.
1769. Translation into blank verse, by Thornton and Warner. 5 vols.
1804. Schmieder. 2 vols.
1809. Bothe. 4 vols. in 2.
1829. Valpy's reprint of the Delphin edition. 4 vols.
1877. Tauchnitz. Text only. 4 vols.

The best commentary for general use is Taubmann's. The explanatory notes of Lambinus are good, and Valpy's reprint of the Delphin contains a full index, and all the Variorum notes with some others by the editor.

The following editions contain one or more plays. Only those which have explanatory notes are given: —

1830. Lindemann. Captivi, Trinummus. Amphitruo. Sold separately.
1836–9. Hildyard. Menaechmei, Aulularia. 2 vols.
1848–53. Ritschl. Vol. I. Prolegomena, Trinummus, Miles Gloriosus, Bacchides. Vol. II. Stichus, Pseudolus, Menaechmi, Mostellaria. Vol. III. Part I. Persa, Mercator.
1864. Brix. Trinummus, Captivi, Menaechmi. Sold separately.
1866–76. Lorenz. Mostellaria, Miles Gloriosus, Pseudolus. 3 vols.
1869. Ramsay. Mostellaria.
1875–6. Wagner, Wilhelm. Trinummus, Aulularia. 2 vols.
1879. Sonnenschein.

Of these Ritschl's edition is the most valuable. Hildyard has Latin notes and an excellent Glossary, with index, but the text is not good. Brix and Lorenz have full and very good German notes. Wagner's plays are the best in English for the college student. Sonnenschein's Captivi is an English translation of the edition of Brix, with some additional notes. For the student who has read two or three plays, Ramsay's Mostellaria, though it is incomplete and leaves many points untouched, is by far the best English edition.

Explanations of the metre and prosody of Plautus are given by Wagner (Aul.), Ramsay, Brix (Trin.), and Sonnenschein. More extended statements will be found in the Prolegomena to Ritschl's Trinummus and in Hermann's Elementa (or Epitome) Doctrinae Metricae. All these are largely indebted to the De Metris Terentianis Schediasma, prefixed to Bentley's Terence.

INDEX.

abhinc, with abl., II. 2. 63.
accersunt, II. 2. 76.
Acc. plu. in *-is*, *-es* or *-eis*, I. 1. 6.
Active for depon. verbs, I. 3. 10, II. 1. 24.
adaeque, I. 1. 29.
ad me ad cenam, V. 3. 13.
ad portum, II. 1. 5.
adulescens, III. 1. 118.
advorsitor, Dram. Pers.
alliato, I. 1. 45.
amabo, I. 3. 10.
amittere = dimittere, II. 2. 2.
an, I. 1. 7.
angiportus, V. 1. 4.
antiquom tuum, III. 2. 100.
apage, II. 2. 6.
aps te cavere, IV. 2. 21.
arraboni, III. 1. 112.
atque, II. 2. 57, III. 2. 138, V. 1. 9.
autem, III. 2. 89.

balineas, III. 2. 67.
bene ambula, III. 2. 164.
benevolens, I. 3. 38.
bucaedae, IV. 1. 25.

c, qu, I. 3. 120.
cantor, V. 3. 59.

capitalis caedis, II. 2. 44.
capiundos crines, I. 3. 69.
captare cum aliquo, V. 2. 6.
caput, I. 3. 54.
carnufex, I. 1. 52.
cavere cum aliquo, V. 3. 21.
cave respexis, II. 2. 89.
cauto opus est, IV. 1. 42.
cedo, I. 3. 91.
cena, II. 2. 53.
certa res est, III. 2. 17.
certum est, I. 3. 80.
cis, I. 1. 17.
clam, with acc., V. 1. 13.
Colloquial language, I. 1. 9.
commeream, V. 3. 56.
comminiscere, III. 1. 127.
compendi facere, I. 1. 57.
concrepuit, II. 2. 74.
congerrones, IV. 2. 27.
cordi, I. 4. 10.
curriculo, II. 1. 15.

da ab aliquo, I. 4. 34.
danisticum, III. 1. 123.
de, "after," III. 2. 8.
decem, I. 3. 81.
defodit insepultum, II. 2. 70.
delicatus, IV. 3. 9.

deliciae popli, I. 1. 14.
detexit, I. 3. 7.
dicam, si confessus sit, III. 1. 24.
die crastini, IV. 1. 22.
di te ament, I. 4. 28.
dormiunt, III. 2. 140.
do tibi operam, III. 2. 115.
duint, III. 1. 120.
dum, enclitic, I. 2. 36.
dum, "until," with indic., III. 1. 148.

eadem opera, IV. 4. 45.
eatenus, I. 2. 46.
ecastor, I. 3. 1.
eccum, I. 1. 79.
edepol, III. 1. 76.
empti fuerant, III. 2. 132.
enim, IV. 1. 30.
eradicitus, V. 2. 48.
euge, I. 3. 103.
examussim, I. 2. 18.
exheres, I. 3. 77.
exin, correl. with *ut*, I. 3. 70.

fabula, IV. 3. 5.
facere lucri, II. 1. 7.
face sient, II. 1. 53.
facetus, I. 1. 43.
facito cogites, I. 3. 59.
faenori, III. 1. 1.
faxo, I. 1. 65.
ferocem facere, IV. 1. 31.
ferratile, I. 1. 18.
Figura etymologica, I. 1. 78, I. 3. 5, I. 3. 27.
flare sorbereque, III. 2. 102.

flocci existumare, I. 1. 73.
flocci facere, III. 2. 119.
foras, I. 1. 1, IV. 4. 12.
Frequentative verbs, I. 1. 51.
frugi, I. 2. 48.
frustra, III. 1. 36.
frutex, I. 1. 12.
fumus, IV. 1. 32.
furcifer, I. 1. 66.
Future indic. in *-so, -sso*, I. 1. 65.
 in a wish, II. 2. 86.
 for imperv., II. 2. 94.
Future perfect for future, I. 3. 54.

Genitive in exclamations, IV. 2. 9.
germana, I. 1. 39.
gnarures esse, I. 2. 16.
gratiis, I. 3. 19.

haec = hae, I. 3. 9.
hariolus, III. 1. 40.
haud, I. 2. 10.
herilis, I. 1. 3.
hoc habet, III. 2. 26.
hocine, I. 1. 9.

igitur, I. 2. 47.
illisce, nom., II. 2. 77.
imo (immo), I. 4. 22.
Impatient or indignant questions, I. 3. 143, II. 1. 36, III. 1. 125, IV. 3. 5, IV. 2. 20, IV. 4. 22.
inconciliare, III. 1. 80.
Indicative in indirect questions, I. 2. 64, I. 3. 42, III. 1. 81.
indignis modis, IV. 4. 39.
in perpetuom modum, III. 1. 5.

INDEX. 157

inpetrabilis, V. 3. 40.
inpluere, with dat. or acc., IV. 1. 13.
insanum, IV. 2. 5.
inservire, with acc., I. 3. 33.
intellego, II. 2. 44.
interdius, II. 2. 14.
intro, I. 3. 136.
intuor, III. 2. 147.
intus, II. 1. 47.
ire infitias, IV. 4. 29.
istanc, I. 3. 106.
ita, I. 1. 53.

largiter, II. 2. 8.
lepidus, I. 3. 14.
licet, II. 1. 55.
ludos alicui facere, II. 1. 79.
ludus fit, Arg.

madeo metu, II. 1. 48.
malum, I. 1, 6, "punishment," IV. 1. 1.
mani, III. 1. 3.
manu emittere, IV. 3. 36.
manumisit, Arg.
med, V. 2. 45.
melius fuit, III. 2. 1.
merenda, IV. 3. 27.
meticulosa, V. 2. 37.
mirum quin, II. 2. 62.
miseris modis, I. 1. 51.
molestus ne sis, I. 1. 71.
morem gerere alicui, I. 3. 32.
morigerae, II. 1. 51.
musice, III. 2. 40.
nauci, V. 1. 1.

ne (nae), IV. 3. 46.
nec, III. 1. 31.
nec recte dicere, I. 3. 83.
ne γρῦ quidem, III. 1. 63.
nequam, I. 2. 21.
ni, II. 1. 67.
nihil enim, III. 1. 20.
nihili, I. 2. 70.
nil moror, III. 2. 57.
nimio, I. 1. 69.
nimis, I. 3. 20.
nimis quam, II. 2. 78.
noli facere, III. 2. 124.
nominare, III. 1. 55.
non forte, III. 2. 5.
non modo ne, II. 1. 43.
nudiustertius, IV. 3. 17.
nullus sum, II. 1. 41.
num non vis, I. 4. 23.
numquid aliud? II. 1. 57.

ocellus, I. 3. 11.
oculi dolent, IV. 1. 32.
olere, I. 1. 41.
operae pretium, III. 2. 154.
opibus atque industriis, II. 1. 1.
oppido, I. 2. 51.
opsecro vostram fidem, I. 1. 74.
optume velle alicui, I. 4. 24.
optumi quisque, I. 2. 69.
orare, III. 1. 147.
orator, V. 3. 5.

παρὰ προσδοκίαν, I. 3. 96, V. 2. 10.
Perfect passive with *fui*, etc., III. 2. 5.
Perfect for present, I. 3. 54.

pergraecamini, I. 1. 21.
perii, I. 1. 9.
perpetuae, I. 2. 62.
perpluont, I. 2. 27.
Philolachetem, I. 4. 5.
Place from which, II. 2. 10.
Plautine and early forms:
    Acheruns, II. 2. 67.
    Aeguptus, II. 2. 10.
    aps, III. 1. 118.
    apscede, I. 1. 7.
    arrabo, III. 1. 112.
    carint, IV. 1. 1.
    carnufex, I. 1. 52.
    cluens, II. 1. 60.
    cocus, I. 3. 120.
    danunt, I. 2. 44.
    deposivit, II. 1. 35.
    dierecte, I. 1. 8.
    discipulina, I. 2. 68.
    donicum, I. 2. 32.
    duce, I. 4. 11.
    duint, III. 1. 120.
    eccum, I. 1. 79.
    enicasso, I. 3. 55.
    existumare, I. 1. 26.
    eumpse, I. 4. 33.
    ferritribaces, II. 1. 9.
    faxit, II. 1. 51.
    faxo, I. 1. 65.
    gratiis, I. 3. 19.
    gumnastica, I. 2. 66.
    harunce, II. 1. 57.
    hocine, I. 1. 9.
    illisce, nom., II. 2. 77.
    indaudiverit, III. 1. 11.
    interbitat, V. 2. 32.
    istuc, I. 1. 55.
    patiunda, I. 1. 46.
    pessum, V. 3. 49.
    plagipatidae, II. 1. 9.
    popli, I. 1. 14.
    pote, I. 3. 99.
    potesse, IV. 4. 23.
    potin', II. 1. 49.
    prosus, I. 3. 149.
    puere, IV. 3. 9.
    pulcre, I. 1. 51.
    quoi, II. 1. 61.
    quoius, I. 2. 5.
    salvom, I. 1. 11.
    scibo, IV. 4. 5.
    techinae, III. 1. 19.
    tetulit, II. 2. 40.
    tradier, I. 1. 16.
    utibilis, IV. 1. 2.
Pluperfect for perfect, I. 3. 54.
postulare, I. 3. 102.
potin' ut, II. 1. 49.
prae quam, IV. 3. 43.
Predicative dative, I. 4. 10.
Present for future, III. 2. 85.
probus, I. 3. 86.
Pronouns freely used, III. 1. 9, V. 3. 33.
pultiphagus opifex, III. 2. 139.
pultare, II. 2. 23.
Puns, II. 1. 28, III. 2. 27.

quaene, III. 2. 50.
quam ut, IV. 1. 9.
quantum potest, III. 2. 69.
qui, I. 1. 55.
quid, I. 1. 6.

quid ago? II. 1. 21.
quid ais tu? quid vis? III. 1. 82
quin, I. 3. 16.
quod agis, id agas, V. 2. 36.
quod lubet, V. 3. 42.
quom, "inasmuch as," I. 1. 28.

rationem puta, I. 3. 141.
ruri, V. 2. 13.

sagina, I. 1. 62.
Salus saluti, II. 1. 4.
satin', I. 1. 73.
satin' habes? II. 1. 42, III. 2. 142.
scelestus, I. 3. 14.
sic face, V. 3. 8.
sincerum, IV. 1. 11.
si possis, III. 2. 149.
sis, I. 1. 1.
Slave punishments, I. 1. 16, 18, 52, III. 2, 54, V. 3. 45.
sollicitat, III. 2. 15.
stabulum confidentiae, II. 1. 3.
sub diu, III. 2. 76.
Synonymous phrases, I. 2. 17.

talentum magnum, III. 1. 111.
ted, II. 1. 18.
tegulae imbricesque, I. 2. 25.
temperi, I. 4. 2.
tempestas, I. 1. 17, I. 2. 24.
Tranium, III. 1. 29.
triduom unum, IV. 3. 19.

u for *y*, I. 2. 66.
vae capiti tuo, IV. 4. 10.
vicem, II. 1. 8.
victitabam volupe, I. 2. 67.
videor, "I think," I. 3. 113, III. 2. 131.
virtute, I. 3. 17.
vivo argento, I. 3. 84.
una opera, I. 3. 102.
ullus, III. 2. 23.
-und in Gerundive, I. 1. 46.
unde = *a quo*, III. 1. 16.
unus, "a, an," III. 1. 142.
voluptas mea, I. 3. 92.
vostrorum, I. 3. 123.
ut gesserit, IV. 4. 25.
ut videas, I. 3. 86.
utrum ... *-ne, an*, III. 1. 146.

Reduced Retail Prices. *June*, 1880.

LIST OF BOOKS
PUBLISHED BY JOHN ALLYN,
30, FRANKLIN STREET, BOSTON.

Abbott. Latin Prose through English Idiom. Rules and Exercises on Latin Prose Composition. By Rev. E. A. Abbott, D.D. 18mo, 205 pages $1.00

Aristophanes. The Acharnians and Knights. Edited by W. C. Green. (*Catena Classicorum*.) 12mo, 210 pages 1.35

—— The Birds. Edited by C. C. Felton, LL.D. New Edition, revised by Prof. W. W. Goodwin. 16mo, 250 pages 1.25

—— The Clouds. Edited by C. C. Felton, LL.D. New Edition, revised by Prof. W. W. Goodwin. 16mo, 250 pages 1.25

Bennett. Easy Latin Stories for Beginners, with Vocabulary and Notes. 16mo 1.00

—— First Latin Writer, with Accidence, Syntax Rules, Progressive Exercises, and Vocabularies. 16mo 1.25

—— First Latin Exercises, being the Exercises with Rules and Vocabularies from his "FIRST LATIN WRITER." 16mo . . . 1.00

—— Second Latin Writer, containing Hints on writing Latin Prose, with 300 Graduated Exercises. 16mo 1.25

Bowen. A Treatise on Logic, or the Laws of Pure Thought. By Francis Bowen, Professor of Moral Philosophy in Harvard University. 12mo, 460 pages 1.75

—— Hamilton's Metaphysics, arranged and abridged for the use of Colleges and Students. By Prof. F. Bowen. 12mo, 570 pages . 1.75

Champlin. Constitution of the United States, with Brief Comments. By J. T. Champlin, LL.D. 16mo, 205 pages 1.00

Chardenal. First French Course, or Rules and Exercises for Beginners. By C. A. Chardenal. 16mo, 220 pages 75

—— Second French Course, or French Syntax and Reader. 16mo, 250 pages 90

—— French Exercises for Advanced Pupils, containing Rules of French Syntax, Exercises on Rules and Idioms, and a Dictionary of Idiomatical Verbs, Sentences, Phrases, and Proverbs. 16mo, 332 pages 1.25

Cicero. Oratio pro Cluentio. Edited by Austin Stickney, Professor in Trinity College. 16mo, 155 pages $0.90

Cooke. First Principles of Chemical Philosophy. By J. P. Cooke, Jr., Professor of Chemistry and Mineralogy in Harvard University. 12mo, 600 pages 3.00

———— Elements of Chemical Physics. By Professor J. P. Cooke, Jr. 8vo, 750 pages 5.00

———— Elementary Chemistry.

Demosthenes. Olynthiacs and Philippics. Edited by W. S. Tyler, Professor of Greek in Amherst College. 16mo, 253 pages. 1.25

Separately. The Olynthiacs. 98 pages 75

The Philippics. 155 pages 90

———— On the Crown. Edited by Arthur Holmes. New Edition, revised by Prof. W. S. Tyler. 16mo, 304 pages 1.50

De Tocqueville. Democracy in America. Translated by Reeve. Revised and edited, with Notes, by Francis Bowen, Professor of Moral Philosophy in Harvard University. Sixth Edition. 2 vols. 8vo 5.00

———— American Institutions. Being a cheaper edition of Vol. I. of the preceding work, and designed for use as a College Text-Book. 12mo, 560 pages 1.60

Felton. Selections from Modern Greek Writers. Edited by C. C. Felton, LL.D. 12mo, 230 pages 1.25

Fernald's Selections from Greek Historians. Edited, with maps, by O. M. Fernald, Professor of Greek in Williams College. 12mo 1.75

Herodotus and Thucydides. Selections. Edited by R. M. Mather, Professor of Greek and German in Amherst College. 16mo 1.00

Homer's Iliad. Books I. to III. Edited by Arthur Sidgwick, M.A., Assistant Master at Rugby, and Robt. P. Keep, Ph.D., Williston Seminary, Easthampton. 16mo 1.00

Horace. With Notes by Macleane, revised and edited by R. H. Chase. 12mo, 580 pages 1.60

Humphreys. Elementary Latin Prose Compostition. By E. R. Humphreys, LL.D.

———— Advanced Latin Prose Composition.

Isocrates. The Panegyricus. Edited by C. C. Felton, LL.D.; new Edition, revised by Prof. W. W. Goodwin. 16mo, 155 pp. . .90

Juvenal. Thirteen Satires. With Notes by Macleane, revised and edited by Samuel Hart, Professor in Trinity College. 16mo, 262 pages $1.25

——— Edited by G. A. Simcox, Queen's College, Oxford. (*Catena Classicorum.*) 12mo, 225 pages 1.50

Kampen. Fifteen maps illustrating Cæsar's Gallic War. Oblong 4to, cloth.

Pennell. History of Ancient Greece to 146 B.C. With Map and Plans. By R. F. Pennell, Professor in Phillips Exeter Academy. 16mo, 130 pages 75

——— History of Ancient Rome to 476 A.D. 16mo, 206 pages . . .75

——— The Latin Subjunctive. A Manual for Preparatory Schools. 16mo, sewed, 56 pages 30

Persius. Edited by Samuel Hart, Professor in Trinity College. 16mo, 91 pages .90

Plato. The Apology and Crito. Edited by W. Wagner, Ph.D. Revised. 16mo, 145 pages 1.00

——— The Phædo. Edited by W. Wagner, Ph.D. 16mo, 200 pages 1.35

Plautus. The Mostellaria, edited by Prof. E. P. Morris, Drury College, Springfield, Mo.

Sharples. Chemical Tables, arranged for Laboratory Use, by S. P. Sharples, S.B. 12mo, 200 pages 2.25

Sophocles. The Ajax. Edited by R. C. Jebb, Trinity College, Cambridge. 12mo, 200 pages 1.25

——— The Electra. Edited by R. C. Jebb. New Edition, revised by Prof. R. H. Mather. 16mo, 230 pages 1.25

Tacitus. Selections. Edited by Dr. J. T. Champlin. 16mo, 272 pages 1.25

Thucydides. Books I., II. Edited by Charles Bigg, Christ Church, Oxford. (*Catena Classicorum.*) 12mo, 360 pages . . . 2.00

Timayenis. The Language of the Greeks, by T. T. Timayenis, Ph.D. 12mo 1.50

——— Æsop's Fables, with Notes and Vocabulary. 16mo 1.50

——— Xenophon's Anabasis, Books I.-IV. With Notes and Vocabulary. 16mo

Xenophon. The Memorabilia. Edited by S. R. Winans, College of New Jersey. 16mo

ARISTOPHANES' BIRDS AND CLOUDS.

THE BIRDS OF ARISTOPHANES. With Notes and a Metrical Table, by C. C. FELTON, LL.D., President of Harvard University. New Edition, revised by W. W. GOODWIN, Eliot Professor of Greek Literature in Harvard University. 12mo, 250 pages. $1.25.

THE CLOUDS OF ARISTOPHANES. With Notes and a Metrical Table, by C. C. FELTON, LL.D. New Edition, revised by Professor W. W. GOODWIN. 12mo, 250 pages. $1.25.

President Felton, by his tastes and his studies, was especially fitted for the difficult task of editing Aristophanes, and the notes of these two books show with what skill and thoroughness the congenial labor has been performed. Great care has been taken to explain the judicial expressions and the frequent allusions to the political and social life of Athens. In the new editions, revised by Professor Goodwin, the commentary has been enlarged by references to his Moods and Tenses of the Greek Verb.

CICERO PRO CLUENTIO.
M. T. Ciceronis pro A. Cluentio Habito Oratio ad Judices. With English Notes, by AUSTIN STICKNEY, A.M., Professor of Latin in Trinity College, Hartford. Fourth Edition. 16mo, 155 pages. 90 cents.

The Notes are designed to supply the student with such information, in respect to the facts of the case and the scope of the argument, as is necessary to the proper understanding of the oration.

DEMOSTHENES' OLYNTHIACS AND PHILIPPICS.
The Olynthiacs and Philippics of Demosthenes. With Introduction and Notes, for the use of Schools and Colleges, by W. S. TYLER, Williston Professor of Greek in Amherst College. 16mo, 256 pages. $1.25.

Separately. THE OLYNTHIACS. 98 pages. 75 cents.
THE PHILIPPICS. 158 pages. 90 cents.

The aim of the editor has been to help the student only where help was needed, to dispense with all *useless* comment, which includes all notes that are *certain not to be used*, and to condense the entire book within the smallest possible compass. The references are to the grammars of Hadley, Curtius, Goodwin, and Crosby. A notable feature of this edition are the general and special introductions, the analyses of the argument, and the summaries prefixed to each division.

We have just finished reading Professor Tyler's Olynthiacs and Philippics, and find the book very serviceable. The annotations are clear and scholarly, and the text is very correct. — *Professor D'Ooge, University of Michigan, Ann Arbor.*

The notes are compact and scholarly, the translations are concise and idiomatic, the difficulties are well explained; in short, the book seems to me, in every way, adapted to the young men and women who read these orations in our American colleges. — *Professor Kerr, University of Wisconsin, Madison.*

DEMOSTHENES ON THE CROWN. The De Corona of Demosthenes. With English Notes by the Rev. ARTHUR HOLMES, M.A., Senior Fellow of Clare College, Cambridge. Revised Edition, by W. S. TYLER, Williston Professor of Greek in Amherst College. 16mo, 304 pages. $1.50.

The text is preceded by an introduction, containing a concise statement of the history of the oration and an analysis of the argument. In the notes the American editor has omitted not a few of the English editor's citations from Greek authors, and whatever else seemed to be superfluous or sure to be neglected by college students and filled their place by references to American grammars and exact, yet idiomatic, translations of difficult passages.

I have already expressed to Professor Tyler my high appreciation of his *De Corona* of Demosthenes, and shall take pleasure in recommending it as the best edition for college use. — *Professor Harkness, Brown University, Providence.*

Professor Tyler's edition of Demosthenes' Oration on the Crown is a great improvement on the English one, both in its additions and its omissions. I know of nothing so well adapted to giving a student the fullest and clearest knowledge of this masterpiece of Greek literature. — *Professor Taylor Lewis, Union College Schenectady.*

FELTON'S GREEK HISTORIANS. Felton's Selections from Greek Historians, arranged in the Order of Events. New Edition, with Notes, by O. M. FERNALD, Professor of Greek in Williams College. With three maps. 12mo. $1.75.

In the new edition, some passages of the old "Selections" have been omitted in order to bring the work within a reasonable compass, though enough has been left for the historical reading of the freshman year in college. The extracts are taken from Diodorus Siculus, Herodotus, Thucydides, and Xenophon. The text has been thoroughly revised. The notes are entirely new, and include nothing of Prof. Felton's, except with acknowledgment. To the notes upon Herodotus has been prefixed a table of the peculiarities of the Ionic Dialect. The references are to Goodwin's and Hadley's grammars, and to Goodwin's Moods and Tenses.

FELTON'S MODERN GREEK. Selections from Modern Greek Writers in Prose and Poetry. With Notes by C. C. FELTON, LL.D., Eliot Professor of Greek Literature in Harvard University 12mo, 230 pages. $1.25.

The object of this volume is to exhibit the present state of the Greek language, as spoken and written by cultivated men, and as it appears in popular poems and ballads. The selections have been limited to a few authors, and to passages which refer to the history and condition of Greece, and which have an interest and value of themselves.

HERODOTUS.   See Mather's Selections.

HORACE.   The Works of Horace, with English Notes, by the Rev. A. J. MACLEANE, M.A. Revised and edited by R. H. CHASE, A.M. 12mo, 580 pages. $1.60.

This edition of Horace is substantially the same with Mr. Macleane's abridgment of his larger edition in the Bibliotheca Classica. The text is unaltered. Only such changes have been made in the notes as seemed necessary to adapt the book to the class room. Discussions respecting the various readings and disputed points have been omitted; the arguments of the Odes have been introduced from the larger work; and Dr. Beck's Introduction to the Metres has been appended to the notes.

ISOCRATES' PANEGYRICUS.   The Panegyricus of Isocrates, from the text of Bremi, with English Notes by C. C. FELTON, LL.D. Third Edition, revised by Professor C. C. GOODWIN. 12mo, 155 pp. 90 cents.

The Panegyricus has been selected for publication, partly because it is an excellent specimen of the best manner of Isocrates, and partly because, by its plan, it presents a review of the history of Athens from the mythical ages down to the period following the treaty of Antalcidas, and is a convenient work to make the text-book for lessons in Greek history. The present edition is by Prof. Goodwin, who has added grammatical and other notes.

JUVENAL.   Thirteen Satires of Juvenal. With English Notes by the Rev. A. J. MACLEANE, M.A., Trinity College, Cambridge. Abridged, with Additions, by the Rev. SAMUEL HART, M.A., Professor in Trinity College, Hartford. 16mo, 262 pages. $1.25.

Macleane's Commentary is highly valued among scholars, but its price has, for the most part, kept it out of the reach of our undergraduates. Professor Hart's abridgment has now put into their hands all that would be of use to them in the larger book. In addition, the editor has incorporated much that is useful from the notes of Heinrich, of Mayor, and of other commentators; and has inserted notes and comments of his own, including many explanations of peculiar construction, and a considerable body of grammatical references.

The work of the American editor is done with excellent judgment, and his additions to the notes will greatly increase their value for our students. — *Professor E. P. Crowell, Amherst College.*

I am happy to say that I have in use Professor Hart's edition of Juvenal, and find it a very useful, judicious, and scholarly manual, admirably adapted to the wants of the class. — *Professor L. Coleman, Lafayette College, Easton.*

JUVENAL. Thirteen Satires of Juvenal, with Notes and Introduction by G. A. SIMCOX, M.A., Fellow of Queen's College, Oxford. Second Edition, revised and enlarged. (*Catena Classicorum.*) 16mo, 225 pages. $1.50.

The text of this edition is mainly that of Jahn; variations are noticed when they occur, and the editor's reasons for the choice are given. The notes are original and scholarly, and are marked by a real desire to place in the hands of the learner all that is most effective to throw light upon the author. The introduction is calculated to give the student much insight into the writings of Juvenal and their relation to his age.

The charm of Mr. Simcox's work lies in the very scholarly character of his notes and their freshness. It will be of great value to those who are glad to avail themselves of a clear and terse annotation. — *Professor F. P. Nash, Hobart College, New York.*

MATHER'S SELECTIONS. Selections from Herodotus and Thucydides. With Notes by R. H. MATHER, Professor of Greek and German in Amherst College. 16mo, 150 pages. $1.00.

The extracts from Herodotus are from the 6th, 7th, and 8th Books, and contain about the amount of that author usually read in a college course. To these is added from Thucydides the Funeral Oration of Pericles. In the notes, the aim has been to supply the wants of the pupil rather than of the teacher, to explain the text, and to give such collateral information as the limited space of a text-book would allow.

Mather's Selections is a most admirable text-book. The notes, both grammatical and historical, are eminently lucid, pertinent, and judicious. I need hardly say I shall use it with my classes. — *Professor N. L. Andrews, Madison University, New York.*

I am pleased with the Selections themselves, because of their exceedingly interesting nature; pleased with the amount selected, because it is just what will be read in a term; pleased with the notes, because of their brevity, pertinence, and comprehensiveness; and now, after using it for the past two years with college classes, I find myself liking it better still. — *Professor W. F. Swahlen, McKendree College, Ohio.*

PERSIUS. The Satires of Persius, with English Notes, based on those of Macleane and Conington, by the Rev. SAMUEL HART, M.A., Professor in Trinity College, Hartford. 16mo, 91 pages. 90 cents.

The text of this edition agrees in most places with that of Jahn. In the arguments prefixed to each satire, the editor has endeavored to give a suggestive outline of the poet's thoughts, and also to point out as clearly as possible, in the notes the connection of one idea, or one part of the poem, with another.

PLATO'S APOLOGY AND CRITO. Plato's Apology of Socrates and Crito, with Notes, critical and exegetical, and a logical Analysis of the Apology, by W. WAGNER, Ph.D. Revised Edition. 16mo, 145 pages. $1.00.

The text of this edition is based on that of the Bodleian MS., and is claimed to be the most correct text extant. Throughout the work, the editor's aim has been to be as brief and concise as possible, not attempting originality, but carefully using and arranging the materials amassed by preceding commentators. In the revised edition, some references to parallel passages have been omitted, and extended references to American grammars have been added.

The text has been prepared with great care, and the print is excellent. . . . The notes show much thought and discrimination. They are apt and terse, and just such as a student needs; the grammatical references to Hadley and Goodwin give this edition a preference over others. — *Prof. F. W. Tustin, University at Lewisburg, Pa.*

I am glad you have republished the book, which, I think, will be useful in this country. The work, like others of Wagner, abounds in original and sensible remarks; the notes are to the point, and tersely expressed. — *Prof. F. D. Allen, University of Cincinnati, Ohio.*

I confidently recommend it to the favorable consideration of all students. It is eminently scholarly without any parade of scholarship, and gives all the requisite information without removing from the student the necessity for using his own brains. — *Prof. H. Whitehouse, Union College, Schenectady.*

PLATO'S PHÆDO. Plato's Phædo, with Notes, Critical and Exegetical, and an Analysis. By WILHELM WAGNER, Ph.D. 16mo, 206 pages. $1.35.

This edition enters especially into the critical and grammatical explanation of the Phædo, and does not profess to exhaust the philosophical thought of the work, least of all to collect the doctrines and tenets of later philosophers and thinkers on the subjects treated by Plato.

I have now in use, with my higher classes, your edition of the Phædo of Plato, and find it altogether satisfactory. It shows much greater care and scholarship than are usually found in college text-books. — *Professor Ch. Morris, Randolph Macon College, Virginia.*

The edition of Plato's Phædo, by Wagner, is one of rare excellence. Seldom, if ever, has there been so much of value in a text-book compressed in so small a space. — *Professor J. Cooper, Rutgers College, New Jersey.*

SOPHOCLES, — THE AJAX. The Ajax of Sophocles. Edited by R. C. JEBB, M.A, Fellow of Trinity College, Cambridge. (*Catena Classicorum.*) 12mo, 206 pages. $1.25.

Mr. Jebb has produced a work which will be read with interest and profit, as it contains, in a compact form, not only a careful summary of the labors of preceding editors, but also many acute and ingenious original remarks. All questions of grammar, construction, and philology, are handled, as they arise, with a helpful and sufficient precision. An exhaustive introduction precedes the play.

www.ingramcontent.com/pod-product-compliance
Lightning Source LLC
Chambersburg PA
CBHW032142160426
43197CB00008B/753